W9-CFI-520

COACHING
EXCELLENCE

By
Dr. Keith Bell

Library of Congress Cataloging-in-Publication Data

Bell, Keith F.
      Coaching excellence / Keith Bell
         p.   cm.
      Includes bibliographical references.
      ISBN 0-945609-03-5 : $19.95
      1. Coaching (Athletics) — Psychological aspects. I. Title.
GV711.B397   1989
796'.07'7 — dc20   85-51524
                                    CIP

10 9 8 7 6 5 4 3 2

This book is available at a special discount when ordered in bulk quantities.

Published and distributed by:
      KEEL PUBLICATIONS
      P.O. Box 200575
      Austin, Texas 78720-0575

In memory of my coach,

Bob "Mr. A" Alexander,

who significantly impacted so many of our lives.

CONTENTS

INTRODUCTION

The Daily Moments Of Truth

They are just fleeting moments, minute chunks of an athlete's life span. They may only last anywhere from a mere 10 seconds to a little over two hours. And they may arrive only once or twice a year, maybe as infrequently as every four years. Yet for an athlete, the major contests are the moments of truth. They are when performance counts. And what counts is performance excellence.

These tests of athletic prowess don't take long, but they are graded on an extremely hard curve. A curve that gets tougher all the time. The competition keeps improving and the level of performance continues to rise. What constituted excellence in the recent past is now only mediocre. And what now is perceived as excellence, begins its drift toward mediocrity at its moment of inception.

As a coach you know that those fleeting moments of performance excellence require an enormous commitment of time and energy to *consistent, high-quality* preparation. Well-timed performance excellence doesn't come easily. It is only through superlative preparation that the quest for excellence is fulfilled.

Your challenges are to get your athletes to put in that consistent, high-quality preparation and to get them to use their preparation when it counts. As a result, your moments of truth arrive every single day, and they linger. You are expected to perform optimally for the duration of every practice session as well as during the contests, not just once or twice a year.

You too must prepare for your performance. It is far too easy to get caught up in your teams' preparation and neglect your own. But, if you are to excel at coaching excellence, you must prepare superlatively.

That's what this book is about. It is intended as a tool for your superlative preparation. It is intended to help you excel at coaching athletes to excellence. It is about coaching excellence.

Any Team Can Win

Every coach has a winning team. Oh, it helps to have the horses, but there is a lot more that goes into victory. It's not always the team with the most talent that wins.

Some teams are blessed with athletes that are naturally more "talented" or better suited for the sport because of their body structures, affinities for rapid motor learning, quick reaction times, or other factors determined by heredity and early development. Nevertheless, no team is blessed with all of the ingredients for success and no team prepares and competes perfectly.

As a result, there is room for any coach to make up for initial deficiences in his athletes' size, speed, skills, experience, and so forth, by doing a better job of developing the available talent. As you know, good intense training and comprehensive preparation promote good performance. You may have to do more with your team, but you always have the opportunity to do so.

Of course, I might be wrong. Perhaps it isn't true that any team can win. But what better belief can you hold? A belief that your team can go all the way helps you to take your team that much further.

THE COACH'S POWER

Power Need Not Be A Bad Word

As a coach you are expected to guide your team and each of its athletes along the path to excellence and victory. Your responsibility is not to do it yourself, but to produce optimal performance in others. That necessitates power.

The word "power" can conjure up all sorts of images of unwanted, exploitative and abusive control of others. I don't use it that way. Power merely refers to the ability of one person to influence change in another person's behavior. As such, power can be truly beneficial as well as abusive.

In any case, power is necessary for a coach to do his job. As University of Alabama at Birmingham basketball coach Gene Bartow proclaims, "Every coach needs a power base..."[1] It is important, therefore, that you become aware of the sources of your power, cultivate them, seize your power bases and use them to affect goal-directed action. You are expected to hold control. And championship coaching requires that you do.

Status

Coaches usually are mandated with total responsibility for their programs. This status is a natural source of power. By the nature of your role you have authority to make virtually all decisions affecting your team. You are expected to tell athletes what to do, when to do it and how to do it. You start with this power. It can be enhanced or eroded depending on your actions.

Status is affected by how you handle your role and how you relate to others. Your power is enhanced by your comfort, confidence and security in your role. Act like you are in control and you will be perceived as being in authority. Professional football coach Bum Phillips, recalling staff meetings during his days as one of Bear Bryant's assistants at Texas A & M, says that he was awed by Bryant's command. "He'd go into a staff meeting and he'd never have to say, 'Let me have you-all's attention.' Hell, he had it. You respected him."[2]

Standing Alone At The Top

A certain degree of autonomy from your employers can be important. Penn State football coach Joe Paterno says, "I don't think any coach can do the job expected of him if he can't have control."[3] A strong owner like George Steinbrenner or Charlie Finley jumping in and calling the shots diminishes the power you have over your athletes. Interference from parents on a parent-run club can similarly erode your authority.

Sometimes in order to function effectively you need to make a stand against such influences. They hired you to do a job. You may have to let them know they need to give you room to do it.

Lonely At The Top

Maintaining some vertical distance from your athletes tends to support your authority. As former baseball manager Earl Weaver says, ". . .a manager can't be buddy-buddy with his players."[4]

Listen to your athletes' problems. Help if you can. But don't lay *your* problems and doubts on your athletes. Problem-solve with, and dump your excess baggage on, your spouse, friends, colleagues and other professionals, but not the players on your team. Neither should you party with your athletes. You're their coach, not their peer.

Vertical distance, however, in no way prevents close communication with athletes regarding team matters. Discuss issues. Consider opinions. Nevertheless, decision-making should remain your province. Former Dodger manager Walter Alston put it this way, "The players get their say. The coaches get their say. Everyone gets their say, but I make the final decisions."[5]

Semi-powerful

Assistant coaches often lack power. Their role leaves them with less decision-making responsibility and authority than the head coach possesses. Final decisions are your province. But just as your position is affected by the actions of the owner or board, your assistants can't do their jobs unless they hold some authority. You must give them responsibility for prescribed situations.

Assistant coaches' power is even further diminished if they are publicly reprimanded or overruled by the head coach. Whenever possible, such discussions should take place in private.

Control Over Opportunity

A major source of a coach's power lies in control over opportunity. You decide who plays, how they play, when they play, where they play and how much they play. As Indiana University basketball coach Bobby Knight says, "We're gonna play basketball my way. We're not going to be democratic here. We're not going to vote on what offense we use. There's no secret. You're either going to play hard, or you're not going to play. That's a great motivating device."

Presumably your athletes are there because they want to participate. You control who will.

It is critically important that your athletes perceive you as willing to use this power. Sometimes you will be tested. It may even become necessary to temporarily or permanently deny one of your better athletes (or even your star) the privilege of training or competing with your team. In fact, this is often the quickest, easiest and most productive way to establish your control and produce goal-oriented action.

Track coach Len Miller relates the following incident regarding American record holding miler Steve Scott:

"One day I shouted at John Koningh, a fine miler who was always about 3% too carefree for my taste. Steve felt I was abusing John. We had hill work scheduled, and I got up above and could hear Steve down below calling me an SOB, defaming me something terrible..."

"I went down the hill and said, 'Who said that?' Steve dutifully raised his hand. 'You're suspended. Talk to you later.' But at the top of the hill he's still there, saying 'Can't I be suspended after the workout?' I said no. And from then on it was the greatest workout I ever saw...for all of them. They knew if I'd suspend Steve, I'd suspend my mother."[6]

The Expert

You are expected to guide your team to the top. You are not expected to do it for them.

You are the expert. You are perceived as holding the secrets to success. You are the prestigious source who, through words and actions, indicates what is good (and how good), what is bad (and how bad), what is acceptable, what is unacceptable and what is likely to yield success. For that matter, to a great extent your athletes look to you to establish what is success.

Being viewed as the expert gives you considerable power. Bum Phillips speaks further of the effect Bear Bryant had upon entering staff meetings, "There'd be 16 of us, counting everybody on the staff, and we'd all be talking. When he'd walk in, everyone would just stop right in the middle of a sentence. . . . He just had that magic about him: if he was going to say anything, you were going to be sure you didn't miss it."[7]

But this power depends on your athletes' estimate of your expertise. When they question the benefit of what you ask them to do, they are more likely to resist. Keeping up in your field is a must. The greater your perceived knowledge and competence, the greater your power.

And of course there is no substitute for success. The more you succeed, the more you are thought to know. Nothing makes you an expert like success.

Commitment

The less effort it requires for you to exercise your power, the greater your power. Power is always relative. It requires the compliance of your athletes.

Your athletes will go along with what you want only if they believe that their goals will be better served by acceding to your power than by resisting. The great majority of the time, this is the case. After all, they probably want to belong to the team; they probably want to participate in the sport; and they probably want to do well. Since you have the power to decide who can participate and usually are perceived as being able to guide them toward excellence, they are likely to choose to do what you ask of them.

With little effort you can generate tremendous cooperation from your athletes by getting them to make a strong commitment to clearly specified team goals. When commitment is high, power is strong. Remind your team that you are engaged in a cooperative pursuit of common goals. They need to know that you are working together toward the same, or similar ends. Discussing this fact helps you and your athletes unite your efforts.

Demonstrate your strong commitment to team goals. Support your athletes' individual goals (when they do not conflict with team goals). Your athletes will then further trust what you say and the intent behind your actions. That trust is an invaluable ingredient for effortless exercise of power. Trust enhances your athletes' willingness to submit to your judgment.

Coercion

Coercive power stems from your athletes' belief that you will punish noncompliance of your directives. Among coaches, coercive power is probably the most commonly exercised form of power – and the costliest.

Make no mistake about it – the exercise of power costs. Athletes tend to resist coercion. When the resistance is strong enough, countercontrol and/or counteraggression are likely to result.

Unfortunately coercion is tantalizing. The attraction is that it seems to work; and to work immediately. When you punish an athlete (or threaten to do so) you usually get immediate cooperation (or promises to do better). That immediate apparent change tells you that your power has worked and leads you toward using coercive efforts to elicit compliance again in the future. The trouble lies in the fact that coercive power tends to work in the short run, but tends not to promote learning, behavior change, or enhanced performance in the long run. . . . And coercion elicits resistance.

When forced to cooperate under the threat of punishment, athletes tend to work to undermine your efforts. They badmouth you to their teammates and criticize your actions; or worse, actively work to hurt the team. This divisive element, at best, is distracting. It draws attention away from goal-oriented action. At worst, it saps at your power. It diminishes your authority, calls into question your expertise, lessens the power of your approval, and erodes commitment.

Coercion has additional costs. It is poor modeling. It produces stress, gets athletes seeking to avoid failure and poor performance, rather than striving to excel and to win, and it undermines enjoyment. Coercive power adds to attrition—and the athletes you lose are not necessarily the bad seeds or the ones that can't cut it. You may lose the superstars, potential superstars, or the athletes that could unite the team; for often, as attempts at coercive influence increase, athletes tend to lose the belief that their behavior is self-controlled. They believe that their successes or failures are caused by their coach. As a result they abdicate their responsibility for success-oriented action. Performance excellence diminishes in value. They lose the potential feelings of accomplishment that could have come with success.

More than one team has failed (and more than one coach has lost his job) because athletes have lost their incentive to play, have stopped playing together, have stubbornly resisted their coach's well-intentioned efforts, have quit or have out-and-out revolted against the coach. In the long run, coercive power is the least effective means of directing your team's actions toward championship performances.

The Hand That Pats The Back

Much of your power has its roots in your athletes' belief that they will be rewarded by following your lead. You are viewed as the expert who holds the secret to success. This perception makes your approval powerful.

You control opportunity. You not only control who plays and when, but you decide which competitions are entered. You oversee preparation and control the game plan. As a result, your actions significantly affect your athletes' opportunity to obtain the rewards of your sport. As baseball manager Frank Robinson so simply observes, "A manager...makes out the line-up card, which determines who will play."[8]

Furthermore, you often control material rewards: the game ball, player-of-the-week certificates, t-shirts, scholarships, bonuses, salary levels, access to the press and public recognition and so forth. Control of these rewards is a significant source of your power over your athletes.

The discriminant presentation of rewards can provide the most efficient and cost-free means of controlling your program. By carefully tying the delivery of rewards (through education, instruction and contingent delivery) to goal-directed action, you provide your athletes with information about what action is desirable, and you provide the incentive for its performance.

Social Strength

Considerable power is generated by a feeling of "being in it together." The social forces on a team are strong. A common cause makes the team that much stronger. Thus the importance of team building.

Peer pressure is not to be overlooked or discounted. Your athletes have a tremendous amount of influence over one another. Tap into this power source, and use it. . . . Or, remove it.

Different Volts For Different Folks

The preferred power source into which to tap varies with the age, experience, sophistication, and goals of the athletes on your team. You will tend to have greater expert power with children than with more experienced and sophisticated athletes. Young athletes will likely have less insight into the connection between training and performance and, therefore, may require more prompting and more external reward.

Your approval will tend to mean less to adolescents when weighed against that of their peers. Meanwhile, experienced athletes may come to devalue the spoils of sport, awards that once were a great source of power over them.

Hey! No one ever said coaching was easy.

With different athletes you will have to devote greater attention to the cultivation of different sources of power. It does make sense, however, to remain aware that your greatest source of power is control over opportunity. View your program as a privilege and a precious opportunity and act consistent with that view.

THE CHAMPIONSHIP MISSION

The Coach's Mission

Every team was formed for a reason. The original purpose may have changed through inattention, evolution, a change in ownership or institutional leadership and priorities, economic demands, the influence of the coach and/or athletes, or as the result of some other force. Nevertheless, some purpose lies at the team's foundation.

Every team has a mission. At the time you were hired, you may have been given a specific mission to fulfill. You might not have. A coach's role, however, is to guide a team toward the fulfillment of the team's purpose. To do your job, you need to know the nature of your mission.

If not mandated with a specific mission, you must discover or create some purpose for your job. It pays to have a *clear statement of purpose*. Such clarity helps you set priorities, make good choices, stay on track and minimize conflicts.

Winning

The goal of any sport is to win. Football coach George Allen suggests that, "In sports the only measure of success is victory.". . ."Winning is the only true goal."[9] Other top notch football coaches echo this sentiment. Paul Brown says, "I play the game to win."[10] George Halas took this idea even further, declaring "I play to win. I always have played to win. I always shall play to win. I speak no praise for the good loser, the man who says, 'Well, I did my best.' "[11]

In his book, *Target On Gold,* Bell (1983) suggests that "Victory, and the competition faced in the quest for that goal, is integral to making [sport] the rich and rewarding pursuit that it is."[12] Clearly, winning is the goal in every sport.

Winning In Its Place

Victory is a goal of tremendous value. The way coach Bobby Knight sees it, "If you're going to play the game, you're going to get more out of it winning."[13]

Winning should be highly valued, not discounted. But winning is the goal of the sport, not necessarily a team's purpose in participation. As Bobby Knight goes on to say, "You could win and still not succeed...And you can lose without really failing at all."[14]

Though the pursuit of victory is almost always integral to fulfilling purpose, winning remains the goal, not the purpose. Winning should not be put above purpose. Neither should winning be so narrowly pursued that purpose is lost.

One of baseball's most fiery competitors and winningest managers, Billy Martin, once observed, "For a long time I couldn't figure out why I got fired as manager in Minnesota. I was a winner there. I finally figured it out. If the owner sours on you, nothing else matters. I'll do anything to win. Winning is my whole life. The only thing is, winning let me down. I always figured that if I won, it didn't matter what else I did. Now I know winning sometimes isn't enough."[15]

Solidly-grounded Action

Although winning is clearly the goal of any sport, the pursuit of victory is not the purpose of choice. Without a doubt, if improperly handled or too narrowly pursued, leading your team to victory can leave you short of fulfilling purpose, distract you from purpose, and even distort the quest.

If the purpose the team's founder, owner or institutional sponsor has in mind is to make money, winning surely will help; but boring games and empty victories against unworthy opponents might not get the job done. If the furtherance of national or institutional pride is desired, victory may be essential; but the way your athletes comport themselves also may be of critical importance. If a community has formed a youth league to keep its children involved, physically fit, and learning personal skills; winning remains important: but, win or lose, keeping kids on the bench or teaching them to circumvent the rules, can court trouble.

Other purposes need not diminish the value of winning as a goal. In fact, to discount the value of the pursuit of victory in sports is to distort the nature (and impair the value) of the activity. *The goal in any sport is to win!*

A coach must be informed of purpose, however, and act accordingly. You will be mandated with pursuing victory, but you will probably need to concern yourself with other factors as well; whether it be making sure everyone plays, courting the press and other PR work, giving attention to public appearance, watching the budget, and so forth. Coaching excellence requires knowledge of your total mission and action consistent with that team purpose.

Mission Impossible?

Michigan football coach Bo Schembechler once suggested that in bigtime college football a coach need "only" do six things to remain employed:

1. "You have to fill the stadium every Saturday.

2. "Do not violate any NCAA recruiting regulations.
3. "Be sure every student you recruit graduates, although a large percentage of every freshman class does not.
4. "Morally, you and your staff have to be better than anybody else on the faculty. And the students you recruit have to be better morally than the rest of the student body.
5. "Be a strong PR man, especially with the alumni and sometimes with the media.
6. "And then win all your games.

"But, if you only measure up in the first five categories, they'll point to the sixth and fire you."

"Your mission, should you choose to accept it. . ."

The Pursuit Of Excellence

Fortunately there is a purpose that will incorporate winning as the goal, and give it its full due, as well as fully support most any other mission you may be given. That purpose is the pursuit of excellence in your sport.

The pursuit of excellence seems to be the purpose of choice. When conscientiously pursued, excellence engages as does no other target.

The pursuit of excellence necessitates high aspirations and concerted effort, key ingredients, not only for producing victory, but for fulfilling a wide variety of other purposes. As a result, action in the pursuit of excellence promotes enjoyment; physical conditioning; skill acquisition; recognition; media, fan, and alumni support; national pride; and a preponderance of black ink. The quest for excellence tends to take care of these missions (and almost any other desirable purpose), often even better than when they are more directly and narrowly pursued.

There are other ways to win, make profits, foster enjoyment and skill acquisition, promote national pride, enhance fitness and better public relations. But in competitive sports, these purposes are best realized by pointing your team in the right direction: training and competing to win, striving for victory and *excellence*!

Programmed Fun

Enjoyment is one of the truly great benefits of sports. "To have fun," however, is not the purpose of choice. "The pursuit of excellence" offers more benefits as the overriding purpose in sports. And "winning" must remain the overriding goal.

At any rate, enjoyment most often comes as a byproduct of other pursuits. Secretary of Education William Bennett once likened "happiness" to a cat. "If you try to coax it or call it," he said, "it will avoid you. It will never come. But if you pay no attention to it and go about your business, you'll find it rubbing against your legs and jumping into your lap." So too is enjoyment like a cat. The fun comes from being engaged in the quest for excellence.

This doesn't mean, however, that enjoyment doesn't warrant a coach's attention. It does. Athletes tend to perform better when they are having fun. And they tend to have more fun when excelling. Whatever you do, it only makes sense to make it fun. Why not make the chase enjoyable?

GOAL SETTING

Begin With Identifying The End

Goals differ from purpose in that purpose is ongoing while goals have definite end points. The team's mission provides the underlying commonality for which the team is formed and maintained. Team goals provide more immediate objectives that serve to keep the team on track and moving toward the realization of it's mission.

Coaching excellence calls for setting clearly defined goals, then devising a plan of action that specifies the most efficient, enjoyable way of reaching those identified goals. Once you know your mission, you can start the goal-setting process.

Aimless Flight

George Halas suggested that, "Before it is possible to achieve anything, an objective must be set. Many people flounder about in life because they do not have a purpose, an objective toward which to work."[16]

Don't leave your team directionless. You must set team goals.

Performance-oriented

Team goals are a necessity for successful coaching. Not just any goals will do, however. Team goals must conform with team purpose and they must be oriented toward performance.

Sports are structured around performance goals. Performance goals provide the excuse for the game, and, to a very large extent, provide the challenge and excitement that makes sports so attractive. It does not matter whether team purpose is to provide an opportunity for recreational enjoyment, to foster the acquisition of personal skills, to build character or the recommended pursuit of excellence in your sport. Team goals must embrace the object of the sport (victory) and be stated in terms of performance objectives.

Selecting The Yellow Brick Road

Though one of the most important functions served by goals is to provide direction, clearly identified goals do not necessarily point the way to the best plan of action. Team purpose must be taken into account, for there are many different routes to the same destination.

Just as you could drive directly to where you are going or take the scenic route, exceed the speed limit and drive through the night or stop to visit friends; so too can you approach your quest for victory in many different fashions. There are trade-offs to be made. You must consider your timetable. Opportunity will be limited. Some situations will better allow for sidetrips, pauses to take in the view and greater exploration. No matter what the situation, however, team purpose must remain paramount.

Keep attuned to purpose. Victory will always be the goal in sports, but the chase may very well be more important than the catch. You want your athletes (and you) to find the experience continually enjoyable and rewarding. You don't want your athletes to burn out. And you don't want to get so focused on the goal (winning) that you lose sight of purpose (the pursuit of excellence) and end up falling into a "winning at all costs ethic" (or lack of ethics!).

Such myopic pursuit of victory distorts the quest. It leads to abuse of the rules and the opportunity. It causes people to lose perspective. And, it only provides for a hollow victory: one without the true rewards awaiting the victor in proper pursuit; the mere appearance of success without success at all.

Triple-charged

As a coach, you are charged with the triple responsibility of leading the selection of team goals, guiding your athletes and assistant coaches toward the selection of individual goals and setting goals for yourself. Furthermore, it is your responsiblity to see that team goals, team members' goals and your goals all conform with team purpose.

Team Astrology: Aligning The Stars

Once team goals have been set, all athletes should be made aware of what their roles can be and how they can contribute. This way team members can then be guided in setting individual goals that will contribute to the team's success.

This does not preclude athletes from setting individual goals other than those directed toward contributing directly to team goals. Individual honors, awards, scholarships, lucrative contracts and the like are all significant in the world of competitive sports. Athletes should be encouraged to seek out such spoils. But a coach's first responsiblity is to the team. You must see to it that athletes only seek those individual goals that do not interfere with team goals and team purpose.

If you do not, many athletes will act in their own best interest, even when such action is not in the best interest of the team. And unfortunately, sometimes an athlete's best interest and that of the team conflict. For example, minor league baseball player Bobby Mitchell admits, "The importance of winning in the minor leagues is somewhat conditional. If you're playing, it's of great concern; if you aren't, ambivalent feelings inevitably arise. The continuation of a career is based solely on one's capacity to get in a lineup and contribute to the success of the team. Bottom line? If the team is winning without you, butt calluses are bound to develop."[17]

Even when no clear conflict exists, some athletes can be expected to place their own goals above team goals. As Los Angeles Dodger outfielder, Ken Landreaux put it, "Winning isn't as important as doing well individually. You can't take teamwork up to the front office to negotiate."

Unless everyone involved aligns their efforts in the active pursuit of team goals and team purpose, the team may not succeed, no matter how superlative are individual performances. Furthermore, as long as crosspurposes exist, conflicts and distractions are sure to arise. It is the coach's job to see that *all* the players' goals are aligned with the team effort, the subs as well as the stars.

You're There Too

You are charged with responsiblity for your team. You are held accountable for your team's performance. No wonder most of your time is devoted to striving to optimize your athletes' performance and to making their athletic experiences rich and rewarding. Yet as a result, you may get so focused on team goals and what is best for your athletes that you neglect to set goals for yourself or, if you set them, to actively pursue them.

Your goals are important. Set them. Pay attention to them. Go after them.

Self-directed Coaching

Coaches have become increasingly aware of the importance and benefits of goal setting. Goal setting, that is, for their team and their athletes. But how many of you carefully establish and actively pursue goals for yourself: goals for your career and goals for your role in the team's pursuit of excellence in your sport?

Why not give your career the same attention and importance you give to your team's success?...Don't get me wrong. Your team's success is likely to play a major role in your job satisfaction and career advancement. Winning must remain a highly valued goal and excellence your mission. But there are many things that you can do within the boundaries of the quest for excellence that will directly add to your coaching pleasure and your career progress.

Similarly, it is easy to get so caught up in preparing for victory that you neglect to focus, in any kind of planned and systematic way, on the things you can do to make it happen.

Your training and experience help keep you moving in the right direction. But would you be content for your athletes to approach their arena armed solely with a good background, a general plan and the desire to do well? Or would you prefer that they also had specific objectives and a carefully devised plan of action to take with them into battle? Don't just push from the rear. Look where you're going.

Up The Ladder

Are you making the kind of money you want to make? Do you have the kind of facility, financial, and personnel support you need to do the kind of job you want to do? Are you spending your time in the kind of activities you enjoy? Are you interested in making a move: do you want to go from high school to college coaching, from coaching to sports administration, from coaching a parent-run club to having your own team? Are you getting the recognition you deserve for your work? What do you want to be doing and what do you want to have accomplished (and why?) in

ten years?...What kind of goals do you have for your career?
...And most importantly what are you doing about them?

The nature of your job makes team performance goals critical. How well your team does will impact your career substantially. It definitely makes sense to place major emphasis on what you can do to enhance your team's performance. But there are additional things you can do to directly aid your career without jeopardizing your team's success or interfering with your prescribed mission. And you should set goals for doing them.

Are you cultivating contacts? Do you request what you want (raises, equipment, assistants, and so on)? Are you setting aside time for reading, courses, conferences or similar activities that will enhance your skills and knowledge base? Are you pursuing credentials that will make you more marketable? Are you politically or otherwise active in professional organizations?

Get clear on what you want in your career. Ask yourself what it is going to take and what is likely to be the best course to pursue. Then devise an action plan complete with short-term and long-term goals to help you achieve your objectives.

Writing Your Script

If you are like most coaches, you have spent a great deal of time planning exactly what you want your athletes to do in practice sessions in order to insure optimal conditioning and preparation. Hopefully, you also have made sure your athletes have learned the principles of goal setting; guided them through setting long-term, intermediary and daily and weekly goals and helped them to put their goals to work for them. But you probably have neglected to set goals for your role in making the successful attainment of team goals a reality. Instead, you have gone about taking care of the coach's business in a far less systematic way than you would ever allow your athletes to train and compete.

Have you set goals for your recruiting (e.g., the minimum number of contacts you want to make this week)? Have you set goals for your contribution to team building (e.g., to compliment at least three players for their supportive action in practice this week)? Have you set goals for making training more fun (e.g., to introduce at least two novel training drills this week, to set up at least two practice routines as competitions, to remind each team member at least once this week that it is his individual responsibility to make practices fun)? If not, now is the time to do so.

It's All The Same

Whether setting goals for your career, team goals, your role in helping your athletes set their goals or establishing goals for your preparation of the team; the process is the same. Long-term and seasonal goals (consistent with team purpose) should be selected. Then you should estimate what it will take to reach the desired destination (some standards of performance: number of victories, number of points scored, etc.) and the likely ingredients for success (speed, teamwork, power/strength, flexiblity, strategy, endurance, performance under pressure, skill, a supportive environment, health, eligiblity, and so forth). Finally, you should devise an action plan for producing those ingredients, one likely to pave the road to success, complete with daily, weekly and intermediary goals to serve as signposts along the way.

Mapping The Way

Once you have identified what it is going to take to have a successful season and have identified the likely ingredients for success, you should write the recipe for team success by constructing a general season-long plan.

Your seasonal planning should consist of an outline of approximately how much time (and when) you plan to devote to the development of each of the ingredients of success and the proper sequence and mixture of training that will lead to the most thorough preparation for your season. Finally, you should devise an action plan, pinpointing specific drills to be done and standards of performance to be met each week. This will serve as a rough outline. Reassess it periodically. Adjust it as needed to accommodate actual levels of performance and evolving opportunity.

Near-sighted

The weekly and daily goals you set will be the most important. They will need to be based on longer-term objectives. But once set, these short-term goals should be the major focus of attention for all concerned. They are the only goals you can do anything about at any given moment. As each opportunity presents itself, it becomes the only one available. The entire team must make the most of it.

Well-constructed Targets

Goals work best when they have the following characteristics:

- **Goals should be expressed as clearly specified behaviors to be performed.** They should be stated in terms of action, not vague states of being or consequences of the action to be performed. A good goal leaves little room for misinterpretation of what is to be done.
- **Goals should be expressed positively.** A good goal describes what to do, rather than what not to do.

- **Goals should be measurable.** A good goal depicts distinct end points that can be assessed for success or failure through the comparison to some set standard.
- **Goals should be quantified.** A good goal has a number attached to it, numerically defining a standard to be achieved. Specified standards are critical. Too often athletes set their goals based on how they feel and how they are doing at that moment, instead of based on some absolute standard.
- **Goals should be time-limited.** A good goal specifies a time by when the goal will be achieved.
- **Goals should specify a standard of performance that provides a reasonable probability of success.** A good goal depicts standards that have been based on levels of past performance and an extrapolation based on the past rate of improvement. The desirable probability of success varies around 50% with higher estimated probabilities being more desirable when the perceived past rates of success are low and lower estimated probabilities being more desirable when the success rate is perceived as having been high.
- **Goals should be open-ended.** A good goal sets an objective to perform *at least* as well as some identified standard; thereby providing a reasonable probability of success without limiting performance.
- **Goals should be set for the full range of activity.** A good sequence of goals discourages premature celebration and the subsequent letdowns that frequently keep teams that get to the championship for the first time from winning. It promotes readiness for the next step on the road to success.
- **Goals rarely should be perfectionistic.** A good goal points toward excellence without demanding perfect performance.

Looking Ahead

3:09 remained to play when S.M.U. scored to come within one point of Arkansas. Bobby Collins never hesitated, ordering a one-point extra point try. A tie would guarantee S.M.U. a piece of the Southwest Conference championship and a trip to the Cotton Bowl: their two goals for the 1982 football season.

S.M.U. scored the point and reached its goals. Unfortunately the tie blemished an otherwise perfect record and cost S.M.U. the national championship. One can only speculate as to how unhesitatingly the decision to go for the one-point conversion would have been made had the national championship been an identified goal. Not that a conference championship and the accompanying trip to the Cotton Bowl were not goals worth setting and striving toward. But it pays to look beyond your goals ✓ and identify what you want to shoot for after you reach your goals.

Most teams do a poor job in this regard. How many teams set their goal to make it to the Super Bowl, then lose it the first time there? Getting there is quite an accomplishment. Only two teams make it each year. But most teams set their goal to make it with little thought of what they are going to do when they get there. Thus, when they win the playoff game that assures goal acquisition, they celebrate as if their season were over. And, in a sense, it is. It's only after they get to the Super Bowl and get beat that they think about setting their goal beyond "getting there" and set their sights on winning the next time out. As Washington Redskin Coach Joe Gibbs reported at the start of the 1984 NFL season (following Washington's 1984 Super Bowl loss to the L.A. Raiders), "I added one thing in my talk to the team this year. I said, 'We also want to win the Super Bowl once we get there.' "

It's truly a rare team that focuses its sights on an immediate goal, but is prepared for the next step on the continuing road to excellence when they succeed. Concentrate your efforts on your immediate objectives, but look ahead enough to forestall a premature end to your team's season, one that can leave your team falling short of achievements that might otherwise be readily within its grasp—like a National Championship!

Nothing Less

The pursuit of excellence is bolstered by high standards. Low aspirations interfere with performance. Set your goals high.

Joe Paterno suggests that, "A coach has to set high goals. He has to aim high, think big and then make sure that his players aspire to the highest goals they can achieve."[18]Bill Walsh agrees. He speaks of the important role the pursuit of high standards of performance played in turning the San Francisco 49ers into Super Bowl champions. "We didn't talk about winning at first, in 1979, when we were 2 and 14," he says. "We talked about improving our standards.... If the standards are there, performance will be able to rise."[19]

You Can't Hitchhike To The Top

You cannot let your athletes get satisfied (or rewarded) too easily and promote excellence at the same time. If they feel good about (or get rewarded for) mediocre performances, where is the motivation to excel?

I recently consulted with a high school coach who wanted to take a team that had been complacent with mediocrity and give it a thirst for excellence. He felt he had made a lot of progress in his first year; exposing them to a much more demanding training schedule and bringing in some successful athletes to model a more diligent approach to training than they had seen before.

Now as the regional championships approached he was faced with a difficult decision. There were qualifying standards that had to be met for athletes to be eligible to compete in the championships. Each team, however, was allowed two competitors per event, even if no one on the team had met standards.

The question that arose was whether he should fill a vacant slot with a freshman who would benefit from the experience or a faster senior, neither of whom had made standards. I suggested that if he were truly interested in raising his team's standards, he might consider doing neither, instead making it policy that no one get a free ride. They would have to meet the qualifying standards to earn a chance to compete.

Announcements That Solidify Dreams

I sometimes hear it suggested that goals are personal matters and should be kept private. Well, that doesn't work well, especially on a team.

Publicly available goals better enable teammates to support, encourage, and applaud one another's goal-directed action. If they do not know where each other is going, and what levels of performance are on track, how can they help each other?

Furthermore, a goal that is to be made public tends to receive greater care and elicit a stronger commitment. Privately held goals need not be as carefully formulated. Nor do they tend to elicit as concerted action, for no one notices when no action is taken on these private intentions. All too often they tend to remain fantasies, wishes and dreams that fail to get pursued.

It is true that when athletes make their goals public knowledge, other athletes might ridicule such goals or the athletes who voice their goals. That truly is a problem. But the problem lies with a team climate that is so oblivious to team purpose that it permits such ridicule, not with the open expression of goals. Moreover, if your team atmosphere supports such behavior, then in fact it becomes even more important that goals get publicly expressed. You need to know that team convention is failing to conform to team purpose so that you can take corrective action.

Get your athletes to make their goals public. Suggest they post them (on the team bulletin board, in the locker room, or on some similar visually available site) for all to see. Encourage them to talk about their goals as they pursue them. And make sure you have a team atmosphere that supports each athlete's action in the quest.

CHAMPIONSHIP COMMUNICATION

Reach Out And Touch Someone

Amos Alonzo Stagg used to say, "No coach ever won a game by what he knows; it's what his players have learned." You don't get to play. Clearly what counts is how well you can get your athletes to perform. That measure of coaching excellence is largely dependent upon how well you communicate with your athletes.

What you have to say to your athletes is critical. The information you convey provides them with the expertise needed to organize and guide their play. Often equally important, however, is how you say what you say, when you say it, whether you have their attention, whether they are willing to listen, how much they trust your word and your expertise and what the message you meant to send means to them. Like the well-thrown pass that only counts if it is caught by a player on the same team, your message must not only be well conceived, but received and understood.

Impartial Treatment

An athlete's willingness to follow your instructions, comply with your commands and accept your advice will be affected by his view of your relationship. If he perceives you as a trusted ally together with whom he pursues common goals, he will be anxious to hear what you have to say and to make good use of what you have to offer.

Trust is important. Your athletes must trust that you are on their side and will act in the team's (and their) best interest. The development of that trust will greatly depend on how you use (or abuse) your power and authority.

Athletes are all unique individuals, and situations vary. So as Bear Bryant professed, "You can't treat them all equal, but you can treat them fairly. That goes not just for how they're different as individuals, but how they're different from other generations."[20]

Going With The Flow

A coach can't live in the past. He must keep abreast of the latest techniques, strategies, scientific advances, equipment, and, if he is to relate to his athletes, even social trends. Joe Paterno suggests that, "The smart ones who can tune themselves in to the new generation are the only ones who will survive. Those who can't," he says, "don't belong in coaching anymore."[21]

Former Boston Celtic coach Red Auerbach thinks a basketball generation lasts six years. He suggests, "By the time that many seasons pass, you've got to change your philosophy. Now I'm not saying that if they go in for disco dancing you have to go in for disco dancing. But you must adjust. Check a lot of good coaches around six years or so. They have a tendency to go down the tube for a while. The smart ones change."[22]

Instructions

Instructions describe, direct, and activate performance. They tell your athletes what to do, how to do it, and when to perform the prescribed action.

Instruction is an extremely effective means of eliciting the desired behavior. Athletes must know what is desired, and/or expected, before they can perform up to expectations. Instructions, however, must be clearly communicated. As Red

Auerbach has said, "The key to coaching is not what you tell 'em, it's what they absorb."[23] They must understand what it is you want them to do, when and where to do it and what standard of performance is desired. Properly relayed, instructions help get these jobs done.

Instructive Timing

Instructions are most effective when delivered immediately prior to performance. Unfortunately, coaches give a lot of their instructions following a performance for which there is no opportunity to repeat. For example, it is most common for a coach to watch closely an athlete's performance during a competition and immediately afterward to tell the athlete what that athlete could do better next time (or even worse, what he did wrong). Unfortunately, the athlete does not have the opportunity to try out the newly prescribed strategy or technique.

Competition is a great time for assessing your athletes' performances, but not necessarily the best time to communicate that assessment. Make note of what you observed while it is fresh in your mind. Often, however, it is better to write it down. Then discuss it with your athletes at a time when they can do something about it, for example, at the next practice or before the next game.

Jim Might Lose, But He's Not A Loser

John is a real worker. Jane is always late. Tom is lazy. Sue is a fighter. Bob gives up when things get tough. Ellen doesn't care enough. Joe is a loner. Jennifer is a team player. Carol is a problem. And Jim is a loser.

Society teaches us to view people as having personality traits, drives, emotions and abilities which explain their behavior.

Though these labels conveniently *describe* wide ranges of behavior, that's all they do: describe behavior. These concepts do not *explain* behavior. Unfortunately, when we act as if given labels cause the behaviors they merely describe, we create pessimism about the prospects for change. Then, labels tend to limit performance, especially when we label people.

Labels put people in boxes. They tend to permanently characterize people with all that the label implies. But labels applied to people are not correct. Labels are static. People are ever changing.

Additionally unfortunate, is the fact that labels are often applied arbitrarily and reflect overgeneralizations. While splashing in a puddle would hardly make someone a "bird," being slow to get a joke can sure make someone a "turkey." One poor performance can make someone "over the hill." And losing a close race can pin someone for life with the label of having "no guts."

Labeling and rating your athletes' performances can help give them direction. They need to know when and how to change their behavior. Labeling your athletes has less value. These labels make change less likely. When you label your athletes, you expect them to act in a manner consistent with the labels you give them and they tend to live up to your expectations.

It may be conversationally convenient to suggest that "Ellen doesn't care enough," when she missed two practices this week. But such labeling has its hazards. The problem with labeling people arises when you decide that Ellen missed two practices this week *because* she "doesn't care enough," instead of remembering that what you really meant by "Ellen doesn't care enough" is merely that she "missed two practices this week." Then you may begin to expect Ellen to fail to take full advantage of future training opportunities; and you might write off an athlete who might yet come around.

Don't label your athletes. People have too great a capacity for change to be put in boxes with labels. Stay open to the possibility that your athletes can make changes for the better.

Jim might lose, but that doesn't make him a loser. He might very well win the next time out!

Mining Your Own Backyard

Championship performances are bolstered by the use of all available resources. Yet too many teams let some of their best resources remain untapped because athletes fail to talk to each other, at least about strategies for success.

Some teams have tremendously successful athletes (even the world's best) on their roster, athletes who are handling at least some aspects of their sport extraordinarily well. Unfortunately, it is rare when their teammates ask these athletes how they do it; how they approach various situations; what they think about before, during and after the performance situation and so on. And the better athletes tend not to do any uninvited sharing of this information.

Encourage your athletes to talk to each other. Get them to help each other out. They truly speak each other's language. Together they can get down to the nitty-gritty of the challenges of their sport.

Talking It Out

How often have you stood on the sidelines at practice and puzzled over "What's wrong with Jane?" Or, after an unusually good effort wondered, "What's gotten into Johnny?"

If it was a good performance, you may have smiled to yourself and thought, "That's the way it should be done." Or, you may have shared your approval with your athlete, praising the effort. A notably poor performance may have elicited your criticism, encouragement or both.

But why not occasionally take it further and use these conspicuously good or bad performances as learning experiences for the entire team? A notably good or poor performance is there for everyone to see. Usually, however, only the performer knows what went into the act. Yet this is tremendously useful information. A group discussion about handling the particular situation in which the notable performance occured can provide benefits for the entire team.

Begin by inviting your athletes to acknowledge their accomplishments. Ask who had a good drill (practice, play, or the like). This inquiry provides your athletes with a chance to get some recognition for their efforts and it tells them that it's okay to feel good about good practice performances.

Then ask them to report what went into their good performance. The information freshly reported by athletes who have just successfully handled the challenges of practice can model strategies for other athletes who either do not have these skills or did not use them. Meanwhile, the act of sharing their successes provides opportunity for these athletes to relive the experience, make note of a job well done and feel good about it. This increases the odds that they will do well again in the future.

Next, ask who had trouble with the drill. (Notice that by putting it this way, you hint that there are obstacles to success that can be overcome, rather than implying that your athletes were, or are, in some way bad or deficient.) This gives your athletes an opportunity to acknowledge that something was hard for them without feeling as if there is something wrong with them.

It is important that the athletes who did poorly talk about their experience. But if this is to happen, such discussion needs to be invited and received in an open, accepting atmosphere. Have fun with their comments. Treat their difficulties as those that are natural parts of the athletic experience. Laugh with them, but see to it that they do not get belittled or laughed at.

Help your athletes identify what went into their failures. But don't stop there. The purpose of such discussions is to help everyone better handle future challenges. As athletes share the difficulty they experienced, ask how they might better handle the next opportunity. Encourage them to get specific about what they might think or do better next time. Then invite additional suggestions. Inquire openly to the group, but also ask selected individuals for ideas. Make sure that everyone understands the suggested strategies and actively participates in the discussion (at least with their thoughts.)

Of particular interest are the thoughts that went on in athletes' heads as they tackled the challenge. These are significant determinants of performance that can't be observed and that are rarely spontaneously reported. An athlete's psychological approach can be improved, however, and should be an object of focus. Discussions such as these can legitimatize athletes' "private worlds" as important areas to be discussed and developed.

Training time is limited and, therefore, precious. And obviously your athletes cannot be conditioning their bodies and practicing their physical skills while they are sitting around talking. But such discussions need not take long and can be time well spent. They can make all other practice time that much more productive.

The Words You Want To Hear

There is a scene in the movie *North Dallas Forty* where wide receiver Phil Elliot is summoned to see B.A., the North Dallas head coach. B.A. takes Phil on a guided tour across the hot coals. He lets into his fading star wide receiver, telling him that the problem is with his "attitude" and his "immaturity." The coach makes it clear to his former starter that the player must adjust to sitting on the bench.

Phil starts to protest, but B.A. clearly refers to his main source of power saying, "If you want to play football for me, Mr. Elliot, you have to change right now." At this point, the player's manner changes and he dutifully tells his coach, "B.A., I'm sorry if my immaturity has offended you. And, I'll honestly try to change. But, I've been a starter for six years and it's hard to sit on the bench. But . . . I'll wait my chance. And when you do start me, I'll make you glad you did."

In the scene described above, the coach gets to hear what he wants to hear. What is said, however, merely completes a ritual, one that gets played out between coach and athlete far too often. Coach tells athlete what is wrong with athlete. Athlete, being no dummy, tells coach what coach wants to hear: an apology and a promise to do better. The coach's anger is appeased. The coach then reinforces the act of atonement and the promise. Of course, what transpires here has little bearing on the behavior of interest. Instead, all that the athlete learns is what to say in this kind of situation. No improvement is made in the athlete's performance.

The next time you confront an athlete with the need for some change on his part and he tells you what you want to hear, let him know that the ritual has been played out: he has said what he thought he was supposed to say. Then, in a very supportive, open manner, invite him to say what he really feels. Maybe together you can get at some solution for the problem at hand.

TEAM BUILDING

Collectively Influenced Individuals

There is no denying the importance of team building. In team sports the games, by their very nature, require cooperative effort. Yet teamwork only comes as the result of the collective contributions of individual team members. Athletes must succeed (or contribute to team success) through their own individual performances. As former Texas football coach Darrell Royal once said, "You talk about *team effort*. What is team effort? Team effort is getting a bunch of individuals ready to play, and then the team plays enthusiastically. But you still have to go back to the individual."[24]

Team performance comes as a direct result of individual execution. So too, however, are individual performances affected by the nature of the team. There exists a reciprocal relationship between player and team climate. Even in the so-called individual sports, athletes neither train or compete in a vacuum. How well they train and how well they compete is significantly influenced by their physical, emotional, cognitive, and social environment; while at the same time, the team environment is shaped continually by what athletes do.

Take care to create a team atmosphere that supports action consistent with team purpose, an atmosphere where the individual is pushed toward contributing to the success of the team. Strive to create a team climate where performance excellence is inevitable.

Team-embraced Purpose

Team building begins with the collective embodiment of a clearly specified team purpose. It is not enough for a coach to have been given a mission, or for a team's purpose to have been clearly determined. Team members must be guided to a clear understanding and adoption of the desired team purpose (hopefully, the pursuit of excellence in your sport). Everyone must be moving together in the same direction.

Consistent, strong adherence to team purpose is difficult enough when everyone involved ascribes to some clearly specified misson. Without a team-embraced mission, however, inattention to purpose, distraction and conflict will result much more often.

A Sense Of Togetherness

You simply could present your mission to the team and let them know they need to embrace the team purpose or find another team. Though such an approach might seem somewhat heavy-handed, it is far preferable to leaving team purpose unidentified. A better sense of "we are all in this together," and a greater commitment to the team's mission, however, is established by enlisting the team's participation in the formulation of a statement of team purpose.

An early season meeting should be devoted to a joint formulation of a clearly stated team pupose. Everyone should participate and everyone must accept the final product. Not everyone must agree that the final statement of purpose perfectly represents the purpose he would have ideally selected. Everyone must, however, agree to embrace the purpose selected.

Tour Guide

Meetings to establish a jointly-embraced team purpose should be facilitated by a leader who is in a position to protect the interests of the team sponsor, as well as the athletes and the coach. Usually this means you or a sports psychologist who has come to prior agreement with you as to the purpose of choice. (If you do choose to avail yourself of a sports psychologist to handle such a meeting, you still should attend the meeting and actively participate.)

A skilled facilitator can expedite the process. And it does need to be expedited. Without skilled leadership, such a meeting can go on indefinitely and never establish an agreed upon statement of team purpose. In addition, a skilled leader can milk the meeting for rich side benefits.

Such meetings can be tremendously informative. When handled properly they not only result in a team-embraced purpose, but also tell you a lot about your athletes.

The Emerging Identity

Most coaches distribute a list of rules and policies to team members. This is an excellent idea. If you have expectations to which you expect your athletes to conform, these expectations need to be communicated to your athletes.

Nevertheless, other conventions and policies also will be formed. Every team establishes its own evolving personality. As things come up, they get handled. Gradually, conventional ways of handling various situations become established as unspoken team policies. These become the team norms. And most everyone follows suit.

Evolutionary Mediocrity

The strongest determinant, and the best predictor, of human behavior is the action of others. People laugh when others laugh.

People applaud when others applaud. Individuals get up and leave a social function when others start to leave. So too, do athletes train better, compete better, and enjoy both more when their teammates do so.

Unfortunately, athletes also tend to goof off in practice, give up in competitions, pick on a team scapegoat, cut each other down, complain about practices and do other goal-detracting things when their teammates do.

Peer pressure acts to create and maintain the conventions that establish the team climate. Left on its own, however, peer pressure rarely, if ever, pushes toward excellence. Instead, it invites conformity and (since an athlete cannot act like one of the crowd and excel at the same time) pushes toward mediocrity.

As a result, team policy tends to naturally evolve in a direction inconsistent with team purpose and supportive of counterproductive behavior (assuming, of course, your team purpose is "the pursuit of excellence" in your sport). Thus, it is no surprise that a coach often falls into the role of policeman trying to protect team purpose and ends up seemingly locked in battle with the very people he is mandated to assist.

Ahmad Rashad, former All Pro wide receiver for the Minnesota Vikings, refers to some of the forces working to erode team purpose. "In a way," he suggests, "a season is always kind of a battle to see if the one thing that holds the team together — trying to win football games—can outlast all the factors that are pulling in the opposite direction."[25] He goes on to identify peer pressure as a major deterring factor. He observes that "peer pressure is very great on teams that are made up of young men."[26] He then provides us with an all too familiar example of peer pressure contributing to what he calls "one of the great unknown comedies of the game": "how few players can carry a play into the game from the sidelines."

Ahmad suggests that one "reason the guy bringing the play in gets it wrong is that he knows—he *knows*—that everyone in the huddle wants him to get it wrong. This is because they always get it wrong when they bring one in. Besides, if anyone screws up on a wrong play, then you can blame the poor sucker who brought it in. So, you get it wrong to satisfy peer pressure. Isn't it wonderful to be in the NFL, at the height of your profession?"[27]

Clearly team policy cannot be left to evolve. It must emerge by design.

Adopting Excellence

As with team purpose, athletes are likely to be most supportive of team policy when they can see the reason behind it and have a hand in formulating it. With proper guidance, a team can jointly specify team policy that will best support team purpose. After team policy and team goals have been established, team policies should be similarly established in a leader-facilitated team meeting.

I recommend that teams be guided toward the adoption of the following team policies:

- Everyone on the team is responsible for the fullfillment of team purpose. Each of us is individually responsible for making the program work for ourselves and for everyone else.
- We accept every team member as a person. His or her right to be on the team and to pursue goals consistent with team purpose is respected at all times. (That includes accepting one's own rights.)
- We place a very high value on the pursuit of excellence and victory. We keep the pursuit of excellence and victory enjoyable. And we help each other out in the quest.
  - We have a high regard for performance excellence, good training and thorough preparation. We support each other's action for excellence. We encourage each other (and ourselves) to do well and to make our sport fun.

And we thank and applaud each other (and ourselves) for contributions to team excellence.

- We welcome difficult, goal-oriented challenges. We seek out challenges that will help us perform better and win. We want to train. And we want to compete. We relish each opportunity.
- We enjoy our sport. On our team we express our enjoyment of training and the competitive situation. We encourage each other to talk about the fun.

- We thank each other (coaches and parents included) for support, encouragement, and appreciation given.

- We express complaints solely to someone who can do something about the problems. When we voice our concerns, we also offer suggestions for corrective action.

- We don't tolerate goal-distracting and goal-detracting behaviors. Our purpose is too important. We recognize, however, that no one is perfect and everyone will mess up from time to time (mostly because he has been inattentive to what he is doing.) Therefore, when someone is acting inconsistently with team purpose, we call his attention to what he is doing and remind him to get back on track.

- When others call our attention to the fact that we are messing up and remind us to get back on track, we appreciate the reminder. Instead of getting embarassed over our inattention to purpose, or viewing a reminder as a personal attack, we thank our teammate for taking the responsibility to help the team. And, we strive to bounce back quickly enough to let our teammate know what we are going to do to get back on track. But at the very least, we express our appreciation for the help and the contribution to the team.

- We have no use for or interest in excuses. We don't need to protect ourselves against others' opinions by making excuses before or after we perform.

The Buck Stops Here

Every athlete must learn that the responsibility for fulfilling team purpose, attaining team goals and reaching his individual goals rests with himself. It can be no other way. As much as a coach might wish to be completely in control, when it comes right down to it, everyone must do his part on his own. Joe Paterno suggests that a coach "must remember that everybody is responsible...it must be a total team effort."[28]

It is encumbent upon you to teach your athletes to be responsible for themselves and to share in the responsibility for making the program work. Athletes must be taught that when the program isn't working, team goals aren't being reached, the team climate is not the best or teammates are failing; it is everyone's responsibility to make things right. When performance is poor, the team is off track, or something is wrong, athletes should be asked: "Is this working?" If the answer is "No," they should be asked: "Whose responsibility is it?" The only acceptable answer to this question should be: "Mine!"

No Puppet On A String

Far too often athletes seem to rely on their coach to make it happen for them. You can't let them do that. If they perceive that their success lies in their coaches' hands, they will be less likely to do well and make a contribution to the team. They also will be less likely to derive any personal gratification from success and, therefore, will be less likely to maintain interest in the sport.

Athletes must learn to perceive the coach as their ally, their advocate, and an expert resource person. They must learn to see you as someone who is in it with them, directing their preparation, and helping them along; but someone who cannot do it for them. Ultimately, success is up to each individual. It is your responsibility to teach that lesson.

Share The Driving

Whenever possible allow your athletes to take responsibility for their role in reaching team goals. Football coach Hugh Campbell insists that, "The head coach's job is to let everybody else show their talents." He says, "If you have great players you have to let them have the freedom to make decisions."[29] He therefore assumes his players are responsible. For example, he doesn't believe in setting a curfew for his players. He suggests that, "You put the responsibility on the guy so he makes the decision when to go to bed, and what generally happens is he appreciates the freedom so much he wants to make it work. . . . I'm of the school that thinks the athlete wants to win as much as I do."[30]

The Unnecessary Push

A good sense of "we are all in this together" (working toward common goals with the same mission) can minimize the need for disciplinary action. You don't need to force athletes into action that they already are commited to take. Nor is that your job.

Bum Phillips says, "My idea of discipline is not makin' guys do something, it's gettin' 'em to do it. There's a difference in bitchin' and coachin'. Some places the whole damn practice is a constant gripe. All negative stuff. The first thing you know is your people tune you out. Then it becomes a challenge to make them do somethin' they should be doin' on their own all along."[31]

Part Of The Team

A sports team is not a social club. Team purpose can be fulfilled without team members liking each other. Everyone on the team does not have to like everyone else. In fact, you can bet that some of the people on your team won't like each other. That's okay. It doesn't matter. What does matter is that everyone on the team accept everyone else: that all team members accept their teammates' right to be there, to participate and to contribute to the team's success.

Every member of the team should be accepted as a person. He should be afforded the respect that will allow him personal integrity and room to pursue his goals (as long as his goals are consistent with team purpose.) This doesn't mean that athletes have to be friends or that they should party together or socialize at all. As L.A. Dodger manager Tommy Lasorda told his players when he took over the team, "I don't care if you don't like [your teammates] off the field, but when you come into this clubhouse I want you to each have one common goal, and that's to win." He says, "I want them to come into the clubhouse and have respect and appreciation for each other. That's the only thing I care about."[32]

A Signigicant Cog

Athletes tend to be acutely tuned-in to the quality of their performance and to their roles on the team. If they are playing poorly or not fitting in as desired, they often get down on themselves, question their abilities, and even doubt their very right to belong, participate and/or contribute. Their doubts often increase in reaction to the criticism they receive in regard to their performance, their attitude, their training habits or their very being, especially when it comes from you. Subsequently, they may deny themselves the minimal respect and rights they expect to be afforded to everyone else.

Particularly vulnerable are the least successful athletes on the team. They are much more likely to be treated as if they have little or nothing to contribute, and to feel that way. If it is true that they have nothing to contribute, they have no place on the team. As long as they remain part of the team, however, they can contribute and they need to know it.

Take care to see that your criticism is well-timed and well-directed. Be sure to *criticize the act, not the person.*

And take care to see that all your players are aware of their right to belong, participate, and contribute. Let them know that each one of them matters. Encourage them to take care of their own rights and to be accepting of themselves, if not always of their performances.

See to it that all of your athletes have clear ideas of their roles and what they can do to contribute to the team. Well-designed and effectively-employed goal setting will go a long way to further everyone's awareness of how he can contribute, and to foster self-acceptance.

More And Tougher

Most athletes tend to talk about practice as if it were a necessary evil—the dues they must pay in order to do well in the game. They tend to ask for shorter practices, easier drills, fewer conditioning exercises, early releases from practice and more days off. They talk as if, except under game conditions, their sport were bad, and more of it were worse.

Of course, few athletes would openly espouse such a philosophy. Their actions, however, tend to loudly proclaim such beliefs.

Excellence is predicated on acceptance of the most difficult challenges. An athlete cannot shy away from the most arduous physical and psychological demands of his sport and expect to produce performance excellence. Yet most teams conventionally do so, and routinely accept each other's diffidence.

Encourage your athletes to welcome the most difficult challenges you present instead of groaning at their introduction, to eagerly tackle these undertakings instead of begrudgingly going through the motions, and to ask for more instead of habitually seeking to avoid the "work." Make it team policy to "go for it."

Deceptive Appearance

Athletes tend to be very concerned with their image. That's not all bad. Projecting the right image can be functional. It can win them a place on the team, make them more money and intimidate opponents. Unfortunately, appearance all too often seems to get put above performance. Then teammates act to drag each other down.

People don't like to look bad. Athletes dislike getting shown up even more than others do. After all, their performance is always judged in the context of others' performances.

Consistent excellence is hard to come by. It is much easier to look good when everyone else is doing poorly. And, perhaps even more influential to practice performance, it is much easier to keep from looking bad when no one on the team is doing anything extraordinarily well. As a result, it seems to be the norm on most teams to discourage anyone from "getting after it," at least in practices. Instead, peer pressure pushes toward mediocrity.

If team purpose is to be fulfilled, however, excellence, enjoyment and team unity must be highly valued. Athletes tend to train better, play better, and enjoy both more when others around them are training well, playing well and having fun. Championship teams push each other to excellence.

Get your team to make it team policy to encourage goal-directed action, to support each other's (and the team's) quest for excellence, and to appreciate and even applaud each other's good performances. Remind them that there is little value in getting to the top of the team if an athlete does so by keeping his teammates down. Even if he manages to con his teammates into poor practice performances, athletes on other teams aren't going to wait around. It's going to catch up to him in the contest. That won't fulfill purpose. After all, what's more important, looking good or doing well?

Championship Sounds

The things you and your athletes say at practice significantly control the social environment, influence values and shape perspectives. If conversation tends to be goal-oriented, optimistic, encouraging, supportive, complimentary of good performance and expressive of the value of the challenge and the joy of the pursuit, the climate tends to be one that nurtures championship performances. On the other hand, if practice conversation is filled with diversion, doubt and discouragement, complaints, criticism and fear, the climate becomes destructive even when such comments are said off-handedly and kiddingly.

What is said should be a continuing focus of a coach's attention. Constructive talk should be encouraged. The doubts, complaints, criticism and expressed fears have no place floating around in the sea of practice conversation. Let your athletes know how important it is that they talk positively about their sports experience. And encourage them to voice their negative feelings only to you, and to do so in private. Let them know that vigilance to what is said is a significant contribution each athlete can make to the team climate.

Athletic Delight

To complain is socially acceptable. To rejoice is considerably less so. When All Star catcher Gary Carter first joined the

Montreal Expos "effusing boyish ardor for everything from batting practice to calisthenics"[33] it grated on some of his teammates. As pitcher Steve Rogers put it, "I thought I was all grown-up. I was at a point where I considered all that youthful enthusiasm misguided."[34]

Part of an athlete's image often is to project "cool." Unfortunately, it doesn't seem to be "cool" these days to enjoy training, to make it fun or to demonstrate enthusiasm and excitement for the job.

Therein lies part of the problem. The sports industry has become such big business that athletics is often viewed as a "job." The fact remains, sports are games. The image sought tends to be one of an aloof, sophisticated, business-like professional. Thus, enjoyment and enthusiasm (at least for practice) tend to get discouraged.

But no matter how much money may be potentially available, and no matter how demanding and serious the pursuit of athletic excellence may be, it only makes sense for your athletes to label your sport as fun, attend to the enjoyable aspects of your sport, openly talk about the fun and creatively make it more fun. Your team could set worse policies.

A Cancer Vaccine

Complaints are cancerous. They eat away at all that's healthy on your team.

Complaints call attention to all that's wrong and undesirable, when attention might just as easily be directed toward the positive aspects of the sports experience. In fact, complaints often make things undesirable by labeling them so. Complaints lend a "bad" label to people, acts and things that might just as well be experienced as helpful, fun, productive, exciting or otherwise "good." When an athlete complains about a practice drill, for example, the complaint starts him, and those teammates within earshot, searching for undesirable aspects of that drill in particular or training in general. If they look hard enough they'll find unpleasantness; or create it.

Admittedly, complaints often have some substance, referring to problems that warrant corrective action. When this is true, it is important that these complaints get expressed. But they are best voiced only to someone able to take corrective action. Teammates don't need to have their attention directed toward that which they are powerless to control.

Complaints are best received when expressed constructively. When suggested solutions accompany complaints, they seem to be directed at improvement rather than appearing to be voiced merely to degrade the program or drag teammates down.

Encourage your team to make it policy to voice their complaints directly to you at an appropriate place and time; and to respond to any complaints they hear on the field or in the locker room with an "I don't want to hear it" and a reminder to make an appointment to speak to the coach. This way you can cut out the cancer before it spreads.

Get On The Stick

It is important for teammates to accept each other. That doesn't mean, however, that they should accept everything each other does. They should not. The coach does not have to be the only person to demonstrate that he cares that things progress in the desired direction. Everyone can contribute to creating a positive team atmosphere and share in the responsibility for getting people back on track when they mess up.

I'm not suggesting that a coach abdicate his responsibility, only that athletes be prompted to recognize theirs.

Peer pressure is a powerful force. Unfortunately, far too often it pushes in the wrong direction. The great teams harness that force and put it to work for them, pushing toward excellence and drawing the train back on the track when it derails.

O.J. Simpson tells us they utilized peer pressure to help each other in their successful years in Buffalo. He says that their coach Lou Sabin told them that, "We don't make any excuses. If a guy isn't going well, you go up and tell him."[35]

We Haven't All Rushed For Over 2000 Yards

Perhaps if an athlete is O.J. Simpson it is easy for him to tactfully tell a teammate to "get on the stick" and have it be okay. For most athletes, however, this isn't easy to do. Their teammates usually don't like to be told that they are screwing up. Nor do they see it as their teammates' place to be telling them. As a result, to call a teammate's attention to his inappropriate behavior or subpar performance is to risk social ostracization, isolation or tension and strained relationships, not to mention probable hostile responses.

Therefore, it pays for a team to get together and make it team policy to answer reminders to get back on track with a "thank you" which would make it safer for athletes to demonstrate their concern for team purpose and a description of what will be done to get back on track which would increase the odds of improved performance.

Suggest such a policy. Wouldn't it be better if your athletes refused to tolerate goal-detracting and goal-distracting behavior and, instead, created a climate where such refusal is not only accepted, but appreciated?

The Power Of Appreciation

It is customary to complain about others' interference. Acts of assistance, however, tend to get acknowledged much less frequently. That's unfortunate, for when athletes support, encourage and applaud their teammates, the team climate becomes more nurturant of excellence. And when athletes let each other know that the aid they have received from each other has been noticed, has helped, and is appreciated, the team gets that much stronger.

It is particularly important that athletes acknowledge each other for action consistent with newly emerging team policy. Old habits die hard, especially ones that have been conventional. Social support for new modes of interaction will hasten their establishment as the norm.

Among teams with younger athletes, policy should include attention to the expression of appreciation for parental support. Parents often are a major source of support and encouragement. Such support, however, tends to be taken for granted. Too bad. It is a rare parent whose backing would not be given more generously and more joyfully, if he knew his efforts were appreciated. Encouraging your athletes to thank their parents for their help can only make your job that much easier.

Nor is there anything wrong with letting your team know that to hear a "thank you" is eminently meaningful to you. They may think it's your job to support and encourage them. But you go far beyond the call of duty. And it doesn't hurt to admit that the sound of your athletes' appreciation for your efforts fuels your fire. Besides, it's good modeling.

Tearing Down The Armor

Doug, a member of my triathlon team, spent six weeks unable to run because of a stress fracture. He kept training in the water and on the bike, but we had to give his leg a chance to heal before he ran.

During the six week period when Doug could not run, there were two triathlons in Texas. At that stage in the sport's history, competitions were not that frequent, especially in Texas where he lived. Doug needed the race experience, but I wasn't about to let him run and risk further injury to his leg or delay to the healing process. We wanted him ready for the Ironman in Hawaii a few months down the road. I did, however, see the decision to take part in the triathlons without doing the runs as opportunities for some good psychological preparation.

Doug tends to get highly competitive. He likes to win. That's great. Unfortunately, like most athletes, I think he has invested too much of his worth in how well he does in athletic competitions. He has tended to judge how good he is by how well he has done. He has tended to view races as opportunities to prove something about himself. And he has tended to worry about how he looks, and what others think.

I saw these upcoming triathlons as opportunities to take action toward breaking the tie between ego and performance. So we planned our strategy.

I asked Doug not to tell anyone about his stress fracture, before, during or after the race. He was to do the swim, the transition from swim to bike, the bike, the transition from bike to run, and then withdraw from the race. He was not to make any excuses. We questioned the need to protect his image of himself in any way. If anyone asked him why he didn't finish (which was likely since he was probably going to be among the leaders until withdrawing from the race), he was to reply, "because I didn't do the run." If asked why he didn't do the run, he was to answer, "because I stopped after the bike." If asked why he stopped after the bike, he planned to reply "because I didn't do the run." His answers would be polite, but of that nature. He did not need to account for his actions to anyone else, nor did he need to make excuses.

"I Did What I Did"

I think it is important to encourage your athletes to divest themselves of their armor by handling pre- and post-performance

63

situations in a fashion similar to the way Doug handled his mid-race withdrawals. They should not offer excuses. Let them experience talking about their performances without putting the results in perspective. They do not have to demonstrate "how good they really are" for anyone.

I suggest that athletes experience answering inquiries as to how well they did after a contest with "I had fun." If it was a race and they are further pressed by "Yeah, but what was your time?", I suggest they answer, "Oh, I had a good time!" When pressed even further, if they wish, they could report their time, but just their time. They don't need to put it in perspective with a "that wasn't very good for me," or a "but I've been a _____(reporting a better time)," let alone an "I was sick last week," "my shoe was untied," or any of the myriad of excuses creatively offered.

There is no utility in making excuses. Athletes do not need to excuse their right to exist when they perform poorly. And they don't need protection against the possibility of doing poorly in an upcoming contest. Poor performances are merely that: poor performances and nothing more. When athletes fail, they merely have performed at less than expectations (theirs and/or other's); they haven't been, and are not bad. They don't need to explain away poor performances.

Why would athletes ever need to make excuses? They wouldn't need to be excused for poor performances unless their worth as a person was determined by how well they do. Excuses are a way of saying, "See that poor performance. That was not typical of me. I am really much better than that. I only failed because of [pick an excuse]."

√ Excuses only impede total commitment and optimal effort. Excuses support a fear of failure that makes it tough to succeed.

√ Excuses are of no use. There should be no place for them on your team.

Additions And Remodeling

The establishment of a clearly defined and unanimously embraced team policy is critical to the formation of a team climate that makes championship performances inevitable. But the formulation of team policy is not a one shot deal, nor is it enough.

I have provided you with some recommended team policies. These (or some variations that address these issues) usually serve well for any team. There exists, however, a myriad of more specific situations that merit explicit policy that I have not addressed. For example, how should a team handle the coach's absence or tardiness, should it occur? What should athletes do after an incomplete (within the alloted time) or failed drill? What is the team's practice policy for inclement weather? These issues and others should be addressed, so that everyone is clear as to what to do should such situations arise.

In addition, policy should be established to handle circumstances that are unique to your sport, your team or your situation. For example, a swimming team might want to establish a policy for handling dragging (drafting off of a swimmer in front) in practice. Some teams experience having an athlete's reaction to his own poor competitive performance infectiously hurt the team. If this is a problem, your team should develop a policy for handling such contingencies. Whatever situations you can identify that are likely to crop up with any frequency, especially if they are likely to affect performance, become prime candidates for a team policy.

No matter how well you assess your team's situation and anticipate future needs, situations will come up that will be better handled by establishing a clear team policy on the matter. The formulation of team policy must be an ongoing process. As things come up, they will get handled. See to it that the team handles them in a way consistent with the team's mission. And use these opportunities to establish a goal-oriented convention for handling similar situations in the future.

Keeping The Ball Rolling

Experience suggests that team meetings that establish clearcut team policy build a stronger team and help to get athletes actively contributing to an exciting and productive team atmosphere. Experience also suggests, however, that unless provisions are made for on-the-field implementation and ongoing maintenance of these policies, the enthusiasm and action that promotes the establishment of a good team climate can gently erode.

Set it up so that team policy will get firmly entrenched in behavior. No matter how good are everyone's intentions, old conventions are hard to change. A good team climate only gets built with continued attention and ongoing maintenance.

Weekly goal setting is an important ingredient for keeping the team going in the right direction. Regularly scheduled team meetings also can help. But make sure that the intentions expressed and agreed upon in team meetings are getting translated into action on the field of play. Many teams have successfully tackled this problem by having the responsibility for encouraging action consistent with particular team policies assumed by individual athletes on a rotating basis.

Team building takes quite a bit of attention, action and maintenance. Getting your team pulling together in the same direction, however, is well worth the effort.

What Do You Do When The Train Gets Derailed?

Critical to the establishment and maintenance of a good team atmosphere is the manner in which noncompliance of team policy gets handled. Provisions must be made for making corrections to deviation from course.

It is not, and should not be, the sole responsibility of the coach to keep the team headed in the right direction. Everyone is affected. And everyone is responsible.

That responsibility is much easier to carry and much more likely to be borne if provisions are made that prescribe how such matters will get handled. For example, although most professional teams (if not all) have team policies that prohibit the use of illicit drugs, there have been quite a few stirrings in professional sports about drug abuse among athletes. You can bet that teammates know of drug use long before the coach does. How should they deal with this knowledge? Whose problems are problems that affect the entire team? How will such problems get handled? These are issues that should get discussed and decisions that best get made.

Team policy will get broken. How these indiscretions get handled can make or break a team.

MOTIVATING YOUR ATHLETES TO TRAIN

No Way To "Will"

Bobby Knight once observed that "We hear about the will to win." Well, he suggested, "The will to win is the most overly exaggerated phenomenon in society. We have to have the will to prepare to win, not the will to win."

Coach Knight's sentiment is well taken. Training and preparation are critical to championship performance. I think, however, we need to take his statement one step further. We don't "have to have the will to prepare to win," we have to prepare to win. I'm not sure "will" has anything to do with it. Certainly it is not to a coach's advantage to assume it does. It may seem as though "where there's a will there's a way," but is there a way to "will?"

"Will" is hard to forge. A coach can more readily plan and control for superlative training and preparation than he can create a "will" that may or may not actually spur good preparation.

Questionless Desire

It is a rare athlete who does not want to do well at his sport. Yet, coaches are prone to question an athlete's "desire" when he fails to give his all. If an athlete "wanted it" badly enough, he would give 110% all the time. Right?...Wrong!

There are many factors that influence an athlete's failure to consistently "put out," probably the least frequent of which is a lack of desire. Athletes more often fail to relentlessly pursue their goals because they:

- lack direction

- see no use in training well
- have little or no incentive to train well
- find training more aversive than rewarding
- get distracted from their goals;
  and/or
- are inattentive to their purpose in training.

When your athletes appear to lack motivation, don't question their desire. You're better off assuming the problem lies in one or more of the above mentioned factors and seeing what you can do to help.

Championship Assumptions

It is the coach's job to provide a climate that will keep the majority of the team consistently "getting after it." That job is aided by embracing a few workable assumptions.

A coach must believe that his athletes are capable of reaching team and individual goals. Success begins with believing that success is possible.

A coach must believe that his athletes want to do well. That belief sets the stage for coach and athlete working together toward common goals. An assumption that an athlete doesn't "want it" leaves you impotent to effect change.

You must assume that the pursuit of excellence and victory is valuable. Otherwise you are playing the wrong game. All sports have an overriding goal: to win. That must be acknowledged. That doesn't mean, however, that one must win in order for the quest to have proved worthwhile. Victory isn't necessary. It is highly desirable. As the outcome of the pursuit its value is limited. As the object of the pursuit its value is limitless.

On Target

People are always motivated. The only question is motivated to do what? If we assume, as is done here, that athletes desire to do well at their sport, the question becomes one of direction, not motivation.

Without goals, athletes have no direction. Even if they have goals, if those goals are not consistent with team goals, their behavior will not reflect the desired motivation. They will head in the wrong direction.

The quest for motivation must begin with the identification of exactly what it is you want your athletes to do. Guide your team through the establishment of a clear statement of team purpose (or a team mission), team goals and individual goals.

Encourage your athletes to set daily and weekly goals for practice performances. Such goals will effectively provide them with the direction and some of the incentive that is necessary to motivate conscientious training and preparation. Training goals help your athletes bridge the gap between training and game performance. They give your athletes something more immediate to shoot for and some criteria for which they can take pride in meeting their everyday performance.

"Want To" Ain't Enough

An educated team is a motivated team. Many athletes, however, are incredibly naive. They fail to understand that consistent, intense training and comprehensive preparation are prerequisites for excellence in modern day athletics. Many of their heads are stuck in an era where natural ability; a modicum of conditioning, strength and skill; and a pile of "want to" in the contest yielded competitive performances. Those days are gone. There are too many talented athletes spending incredibly long hours, intensely and relentlessly taking advantage of the best of the state-of-the-art, scientifically-designed training programs. Certainly in world class competitions it would take the very rarest of talents to be at all competitive without superlative training and preparation.

The physically gifted athletes may have early success with only adequate preparation, but in the long run it catches up with them. Easily attained early success readily interferes with the development of a belief in the need for diligent training. At the highest levels of competition, dedicated practice is a must. Your challenge is to communicate this message to your athletes.

You Know It, But Do They?

Presumably you have formulated a training plan and designed practices based upon your knowledge of exercise physiology, biomechanics, kinesiology, motor learning, sports psychology, and the philosophies and strategies of your sport. To assume your athletes understand the relationships between the drills you ask them to do and these principles is a mistake. Even in this day and age of advanced communications and sophisticated youth, your athletes probably do not share your understanding of what it takes to make a champion. Nevertheless, an understanding of what training routines are intended to accomplish, how that is best done and the likely effects of various training routines makes practice seem more purposeful and meaningful; and it generates greater motivation for training.

Drawing The Connection

Educate your athletes. Teach them the purpose of training and its likely effects. Let them know what you are trying to accomplish and how they can best take advantage of your program.

Obviously the age, educational background, skill level, and experience of your athletes will influence the amount and content of the material you share with them. You cannot talk to a major league All Star professional baseball player who has a Ph.D. in exercise physiology, à la Mike Marshall, in the same way you would explain your program to a little leaguer. Nor would you need to. But you do need to be prepared to answer their questions in a manner understandable and useful to each; and to feel your way through, giving enough of an introduction into your way of doing things to get them motivated to eagerly do it well your way.

If you have done a good job of formulating team purpose and team goals, helped your team members to set good daily and weekly goals (which, of course, necessitates communicating the ingredients for success and what must be done to produce those ingredients), then you have promoted considerable learning in the process. What remains, then, is for you to outline the flow of your season plan, and to clearly communicate some specific principles of training, including:

- The fact that the high level of excellence required in order to be competitive in top notch competitions and the gradual, cumulative nature of the benefits of training make taking advantage of every training opportunity critically important.
- The fact that there is a big difference between capability and probability. (Just because athletes have demonstrated some skill or ability does not necessarily indicate that they can exhibit that strength at will. Athletes must be led to understand that the likelihood of doing it when it counts is largely dependent on the consistency of execution under simulated conditions in practice.)

Competing For Interest

Joe Paterno once observed that, "It isn't enough to tell them that football is the most important thing in their lives and expect them to believe it. With everything that is going on these days you've got to compete for their interest."[36]

The more interesting, exciting, fun, and rewarding you can make goal-oriented practices, the more likely your athletes are to train well. Just as you plan to make practices productive, plan to provide incentive for good training. Plan to:

- Make practice fun.
- Keep your athletes aware of the positive aspects of practice sessions.
- Encourage and provide rewards for training well.

Pay Now, Play Later

People are motivated to do things that they expect will pay off. It is the anticipation that an activity will be enjoyable or that their efforts will be rewarded that spurs people to action.

In general, people exhibit the greatest motivation when they anticipate they will consistently earn immediate rewards when and only when they perform the desired behavior. Yet, it is difficult for athletes to make the connection between their training activities and the payoffs in their sport. And, in fact, there is not a one-to-one correlation between training performance and athletic success. The athlete who trains the best doesn't always win. (Though such preparation surely helps!) There are too many other factors that enter into game performance (not the least of which is heredity) for an athlete to view success as solely dependent on practice performance or, often enough, for an athlete to make much of a connection at all.

Nor does it always seem to be the most consistent practice performances that yield the best game performances. In fact, superlative training tends to mask its own consistency, for it is a complex relationship of all-out training, rest, protection from injury, the development of pace and skill, learning strategy and so forth that leads to excellence. When effort is sacrificed for rest, pace and skill development, it is difficult for an observer to assess the high level of training and preparation taking place.

Sufficient incentive usually exists to motivate athletes to perform well in the contest. The same is not true for the practice situation. Rather, the largest source of motivation for training is the expectancy that it will pay off down the road. Most of that payoff, however, remains tied into the much-delayed and highly uncertain successful tournament performance. There tend to be extremely few, if any, rewards delivered for good practice performances. Unfortunately, too long a delay between actions and their payoffs, as between training and its rewards, can hinder motivation. The successful coach, therefore, strives to make practices more meaningful, more enjoyable, and the occasions for rewarding good training performances.

Time Machines

Inspirational talks, signs, posters and films presented at practice help bring the contests' potentialities of reward psychologically closer in time to the training situation, thereby providing greater incentive value to motivate good practice performances. It occasionally helps to bring in Olympic gold medals, world record certificates, championship rings, trophies, championship banners, or the like, to dangle in front of prospective champions. But these inspirational devices have limited utility, utility which tends to be short-lived. If you employ such devices, change them often.

Pre-payday Payoffs

Provide your athletes with opportunities to receive rewards for good training performances. Purposefully dangled carrots will encourage athletes to set goals for practices, while generating incentive for high quality training performances.

Utilize a variety of inducements and rewards (e.g., athlete of the week awards, raisins or bananas, sports equipment, praise and recognition, and so on). Almost anything works, for it is the information value (of letting your athletes know what is good and when they are on track) that is a major benefit to be derived from the use of such rewards.

Such payoffs lead to self-congratulations. These self-pats on the back, and their accompanying good feelings, help athletes bridge the gap between their training and future competitive performances. And when athletes are pleased with how they handle practice, their interest, enjoyment, confidence and motivation for the sport all increase.

The Ceremonial Gold Star

Publicly delivered praise and rewards are particularly effective for creating an environment rich in incentive for good training. While a mature, successful athlete might not "put out" any extra in practice based on the prospect of earning a box of raisins, he might very well do so if that same box of raisins is to be presented publicly. When so offered, the raisins symbolically represent a job well done. Such rewards are effective.

Many football coaches offer stickers symbolic of performance excellence to be worn on players' helmets. Some coaches offer rewards for the successful completion of demanding conditioning routines. Such rewards further generate self-motivation by adding to the incentive to train well that is already provided by a desire for excellence in the contest.

Whatever Gets Them Through The Night

The rewards and incentives provided for training well should vary. Athletes get tired of the same old gold stars and raisins. They require a variety of incentives.

Some incentives work better for some individuals, and at some times, than others. Just as the threat of a fine often has little power to impact a multimillionaire professional athlete's behavior (other than its effect as a public slap on the wrist) different rewards will generate different amounts of incentive for different athletes. A masters swimmer might revel in the fact that swimming is helping her to stay healthy, trim, well-toned and is providing a welcome diversion to her sedentary job. These inducements may be meaningless to a little leaguer, who might "bust his tail," however, for a box of raisins or some M&Ms. The trick is to establish what is going to work for whom and when.

In advance, you can make some guess as to what rewards might generate the desired training behaviors. But why not ask your athletes for what inducements they are likely to work? Such questioning could save you a lot of time spent in trial and error. Of course, in either case, direct observation of what actually works will point you toward the most effective inducements.

"I Did It!"

Athletes' self-reactions constitute the principal source of reward. When they perform at or above standard, they tend to feel good about what they have done and strive for continued good performance. When they fall short of their training goals they tend to make adjustments toward future improvement (assuming they have done a good job of goal setting).

Your athletes will react to their own performance, especially if training performances are deemed important. They even might kick themselves in the butts. It is a rare athlete, however, who will react publicly to his own job well done.

Public self-criticism is socially accepted and even encouraged. Overt self-praise is socially discouraged. Yet self-congratulations go a long way toward maintaining interest and generating self-motivation.

Encourage your athletes to praise and reward themselves (and each other) for a job well done. And make it okay for the athletes in your program to publicly praise their own actions.

Privileged Play

Act as if participation in your program is a privilege and an exciting opportunity. Remember that the control over opportunity is your greatest source of power and that your sport is a tremendously fun and rewarding pursuit.

You don't need to force your athletes to do anything. (Nor can you.) Encourage them to come to practice. Encourage them to give their all. Communicate your belief that striving to excel and win is the best way to gain the benefits of the experience. And provide them with the opportunity to pursue team goals. You can, however, make that opportunity contingent upon getting with the program: doing what's asked, striving for team goals, and following team rules and policy.

U.C.L.A. basketball coach Larry Farmer says, "Basketball practice is a precious time. If a player misses a class, he doesn't get to practice. If he's late for a tutoring session, he doesn't get to practice. Basketball becomes more and more precious here."[37]

Carrots vs. Threats

The way you offer an opportunity is important. If you tell your athletes that they cannot practice if they cut class, then you have already afforded them the right to train and are threatening to take away that which is already theirs. On the other hand, if you tell them that they may practice if they attend class, then you make continuing participation a privilege they can earn.

This difference in presentation can affect the value athletes attribute to the opportunity to practice. With the first approach they are likely to feel cheated out of something they take for granted. With the second approach they are likely to hold practice more dearly.

The second approach also gets them focused on goal-oriented action. The first approach only gets them focused on doing the very things you want them to avoid.

Not Necessarily A Necessary Evil

Too many athletes fail to make training fun. Instead, they view training as a necessary evil, the sacrifice they must make in order to succeed in the world of sports. In fact, success is likely to require long hours of intense, stressful practice, practice that often is viewed as boring, tiring, painful and a waste of time (time that might otherwise be used to engage in other attractive and worthwhile pursuits). But practice sessions need not be seen that way. They can be viewed as enjoyable.

If you assume your athletes are trying to get out of the "hard work" of training and if you act like a policeman forcing them to do some necessary evil, you only teach and support the belief that practice is the dues that must be paid for success. You effectively tell your athletes that training is something they "have to" do, rather than supporting the reality that they chose to do it, they want to do it and it can be fun. Why do that?

No one, even the most dedicated athlete, eagerly pursues doing something that he "has to" do. People actively resist "have to's." As football coach Tommy Prothro once said, "The time to fear is when it stops being fun."[38]

Why label practice as evil? It has its attractive components.

Assume that your athletes want to do well. Assume your athletes want to immerse themselves in the pursuit of excellence. Assume that inexorable pursuit of excellence is fun.

Making A Game Of Preparing For Games

The main difference between work and play is how the activity is viewed. Nevertheless, you can do much to make your practices more easily enjoyed.

Make intense, goal-oriented training fun. Provide your athletes with goal-directed games, competitions, and challenges. Build novelty and variety into practices.

Notice I recommended that you make "goal-oriented" training fun. You don't want to make your practices fun at the expense of preparation for competitive performance excellence. You want to make the process of preparing for superlative performance enjoyable and exciting.

If so much time is going to be spent on training, it only makes sense to make it fun. Joe Paterno put it this way: "...they ought to have some fun out of playing the game or I had better forget about being a coach."[39]

Tuned To The Good Station

Training offers much opportunity for fun and excitement. But far too often athletes fail to take advantage of the fun inherent in the things you have them do, or even to notice when they are enjoying themselves.

Help your athletes to realize their ability to make any part of training fun. Teach them whose responsibility it is to do so—each individual's!

Direct your athletes' attention to the potential avenues of enjoyment available everyday through training for their sport. Help them to focus on the things they enjoy about practices and the gains they reap from training. Encourage them to talk about the fun. Don't let them discount it.

Want To Whitewash My Fence?

If you want your athletes to be interested in training, to actively seek out the challenges of your sport, to eagerly engage in the pursuit of athletic excellence and to enjoy the quest, you must present your sport and your practices in that light. If your actions, statements and style of presentation reflect your assumptions that training and competing in your sport is fun, rewarding, worth doing and worth more when done well, your athletes will tend to embrace those beliefs.

Get excited about meeting the challenges of your sport. Present practices as exciting challenges to be joyfully tackled. Who knows? If you do, your athletes might just begin to enjoy practice, look forward to it, hate to miss it and eagerly give it all they've got.

Time Off For Good Behavior

In swimming they are called "go-homers," or "get-out" swims. Toward the end of practice, one swimmer is selected to swim a time trial and given a time he must hit. If he swims faster than the goal time, everyone on the team gets to go home. If not, practice continues.

"Go-homers" effectively elicit good, hard efforts. Public performances of this type provide considerable incentive to swim fast. Peer pressure and support increase that incentive considerably.

There are coaches in all sports who employ their form of "go-homers." "Go-homers" are extremely effective. . . . But what exactly do they affect?

In the short run, offering an early release from practice seems to motivate good practice performances. I say "seems to" because I'm not totally convinced that it is not the public nature of the performance and/or the designated importance of good performance on a particular drill, instead of the opportunity to earn the right to go home, that motivates an athlete, or the entire team, to get after it.

When a coach says that if an athlete can achieve some prescribed standard, the team can go home, a situation is created where the athlete is asked to do something which the coach obviously thinks is worthwhile and which reflects a high standard of performance. Furthermore, the athlete is asked to perform publicly before his peers and the coach. I doubt that any additional incentive is needed to motivate performance under these conditions.

Similarly, when a coach says a team can go home if they get a drill right or do it well (or must stay until they do so), the importance of doing that drill right, or well, is clearly communicated. Most often that alone would be enough to motivate performance. In essence, "go-homers" work independently of the incentive to get out of practice and go home.

Unfortunately, "go-homers" are not independent of the incentive to get out and go home. In fact, whether or not such inducements have a motivating effect (or, in any way substantially increase the motivation of an already highly motivating situation), they do label getting out of practice as a reward and they label remaining for the completion of practice, or additional practice, as something aversive to be avoided. In the long run, that's trouble.

If your actions effectively label practice as repugnant, your athletes are also going to view it that way and work to avoid practice. They are going to creatively find all sorts of ways to get out of practice drills, "skate" through them, leave early, or miss practice altogether. If they come to believe training is aversive enough, they may even quit the sport.

Don't make rewards out of times off or early releases from practice. If you do, your athletes might come to think of training like time in jail and getting off like earning parole. Then when they manage to get a reprieve, are they going to want to go back to jail the next day?

A Watched Clock Never Ticks

You want your athletes there when they are at practice. They cannot derive the full benefits of practice if their heads are somewhere else. An athlete busily watching the clock and trying to make it go faster, so that practice will be over and he can get on to whatever it is he is looking forward to (whether it is a hot date, dinner or merely getting away from practice), is not there.

Obviously, if you make training fun, challenging and fully engaging, your athletes are more likely to be there when they are there. There are, however, other steps you can take to keep their heads in the game.

Practices should regularly run for the entire scheduled period of time. If there are reasons to cut them short, try to schedule a shorter practice period in advance. Early releases from practice have little utility. You want your athletes to expect to be there for a certain length of time, rather than hoping they will get out early.

Of course, if you have instilled a good attitude toward training, this is not an issue. They will want to be there and want to have prolonged opportunity to train. But until such perspectives are well-ingrained, firm schedules are important.

Let your athletes know that they should expect to be at practice for a predetermined period of time. Communicate the importance of being there, focused on their training, not watching the clock.

Denied Continuance

I have suggested that "go-homers" depict practice in a very poor light and that practices should run their full term. But should practice never be cut short?

Naturally, there are times when it makes good sense to send your athletes home early. (Notice I said there are times when it makes good sense "to *send* them home early," not "to *let* them go home early.") On occasion you might work with your team on a drill until they get it down. Once they do, you might feel it would be more important for them to rest or experience a change of routine, than to keep going over well-learned plays, or to introduce new strategies and skills at that time. Fine!...But present it to your athletes that way. Even when you you think additional rest might prove more valuable than more practice, make it clear that is what you are doing: providing time to rest as part of optimal use of training time. Don't ever use an early release from practice as a reward.

When it is a good time to stop, let your athletes know that it is, and why. Or, better yet, forbid them the opportunity to continue.

"It Hurts So Good"

You can't threaten your team with "We're going to stay here and repeat it until you get it right!" or, use running laps or doing push-ups as punishment and then expect your athletes to value doing those same drills, running or doing push-ups as part of their quest for excellence. They won't. Use those activities as punishment and they will be viewed as punishing.

Why spoil the fun? Yes, even the most physically demanding challenges can be powerfully exhilirating and tremendously enjoyable. Treat them that way.

Don't make training punishing. Hopefully you won't use threats or punishment at all. If you must use coercive methods, however, employ activities other than the ones needed in preparation for athletic excellence. Keep your sport fun.

Ending Today For Tomorrow

You should strive to make everything about training productive, fun and exciting. It is particularly important, however, that you end practice on a positive note. You want your athletes to leave practice wanting to do more. You want them anxious to return and get after it.

It often is better to make the team leave before you squeeze every last ounce of benefit to be derived from that day's practice. You have to balance today's limited opportunity with an investment in the quality of tomorrow's practice.

A warmdown period may not only prove valuable for physiological reasons, but its contribution to the next day's practice can prove immense. A good warmdown can help your athletes feel cleansed and refreshed, and it can help them to capture that "good kind of tired" that makes them want to come back for more.

A brief relaxation session, complete with strategic reminders of what athletes accomplished and the things they did well in practice, and coupled with suggestions about how good they can choose to feel, how eager they can feel and how much fun they can have in the next practice can work wonders for continued motivation to train. Such sessions are a pleasant way to end practice, and well worth the five to ten minutes of practice time invested.

Mid-stride Imbalance

Indecision paralyzes people. When undecided about whether they want to train, athletes cannot pursue their goals with the relentless vigor they might otherwise exhibit. Unfortunately, athletes tend to act as if they are undecided about decisions they have already made. They waste time and distract themselves from their training while trying over and over again to decide whether they want to train.

Too many athletes all too frequently come into practice asking themselves if they really want to do it. They raise the same issue as they approach drills that might be tough or perceived as boring. But the truth is: they have already decided to compete this season. They have bought the entire program and are now considering requesting refunds on the components. That's foolish. Such action only freezes them in their tracks while they question whether they want to do something they have already decided to do. Pausing in mid-stride only increases the likelihood of falling.

Help your athletes see that their decision to join the team was a commitment to take advantage of every opportunity your program has to offer. Help them see the futility of trying to decide whether to take each step in a journey they have already decided to make. And remind them that *they have already decided to go the route.*

THE COACH'S APPROVAL

The Directive Pat On The Back

Because of your position, expertise, and control over opportunity, your athletes will vigorously pursue your approval. Your praise controls much behavior. Use this power wisely.

The most important function of praise is its information value. Praise serves to effectively guide behavior. Your approval lets your athletes know which of their actions are correct, which performances are worthy of pleasure and which behaviors are appropriate. Your praise helps them determine what's good and when they have done well. . . . It does, that is, when given skillfully at the right moment.

There's Value In Scarcity

Your athletes will work for your approval. But if you approve too often, they have less incentive to persevere.

Praise should be used sparingly. The more often you offer it, the less effective it becomes. If overused it can lose its effectiveness entirely. As long as it remains scarce, praise can serve as a powerful tool with which you can shape and guide behavior.

Molding With Pats

There are times when praise should be handed out frequently. When teaching a new skill or new habits, your praise can mold and solidify behavior. By praising closer and closer approximations to the desired performance, a coach provides the feedback necessary for shaping a skill. In this way, athletes receive information that helps them make adjustments in the right direction. Once the desired behavior emerges, learning progresses best when every correct trial is reinforced until learning is complete.

Keep It Low-key

Teaching technical skills does require frequent praise in the early stages. Nevertheless, it pays to remember that the most important function of this praise is its information value.

Your approval lets your athletes know when they are getting it right. But praise need not be elaborate or effusive. You don't want your athletes to think that their performance is better than it is. A simple, calmly put "that's it," "that's pretty good," "better," or the like will do the job.

Acknowledge a job well done. But omit the "super's," "great's," and other overly enthusiastic and exaggerated praise.

Tougher To Please

Once a skill is learned, performance is better maintained by praising the learned behavior less frequently and less enthusiastically. At this point your praise should become harder-earned, thereby increasing self-motivation.

In order to succeed, your athletes must consistently put out more than they think they can and they must continually strive for heights they might not readily see as attainable. To support their pursuit of excellence, you must offer your praise only for increasingly better levels of performance.

The Good, The Bad, And The Who Knows Which

Praise should be used *judiciously*. Indiscriminate praise lessens its information value.

It is easy to fall into using praise in an attempt to boost an athlete's feelings about himself, to try to get him to like you, or to help him feel better about his performance. But if you label a performance as good when it is not, you fail to help your athlete tell the good from the bad. It's important, therefore, that you have seen your athlete's performance and are sure it was good before you tell him it was.

You are the expert. Your praise lets your athletes know when they are on the right track and are moving in the right direction. Indiscriminate praise leaves your athletes without that guidance.

Be careful about what you praise. You cannot carelessly hand out praise and expect your athletes to "bust" for your approval. You must know what is good for your athletes and only praise that which is good. If everything is good, then nothing is.

"Awesome" Mediocrity

Your words and actions will go a long way toward establishing the standards of performance toward which your team will strive. With your dissatisfaction, pleasure, satisfaction, displeasure and awe, you determine what level of performance and which standards of behavior are good, and which are not. You do so whether by default or intentionally. Do so intentionally!

Use your approval to indicate desirable standards of performance. Only praise performance excellence and movement in that direction. *Don't praise mediocrity.*

If you praise mediocrity, your athletes will strive for and be pleased with mediocre performances. If you praise mediocrity effusively, athletes will be satisfied with mediocrity and be enthusiastic about it.

A mediocre performance called "awesome" only results in lowered standards. Or it strains your credibility. It doesn't encourage excellence.

Success Without Satisfaction

The most successful coaches are never satisfied. They consistently expect more and better from their athletes. They request excellence and relentlessly push their athletes until they get it.

Don't allow yourself to be satisfied with your team's, or team members', performance. If you are satisfied, they will be too. Satisfaction encourages the status quo and fosters complacency. Excellence is nurtured by success without satisfaction. There are always improvements to be made. Even when you get to the top, you need to keep on climbing. San Francisco 49'er coach, Bill Walsh, suggests that players and coaches tend to fall into a "comfort zone" where they are so happy with some achievement that they fail to seek improvement. He suggests that it is the head coach's job to jar others out of such stagnation.[40]

"Ho, Hum"

If you want your athletes to strive for excellence, you cannot afford to get impressed too easily. That is one of the keys to coaching excellence: not to be easily impressed (and never awed) by your players' performances.

If you are impressed too easily, your players will be impressed by their own less-than-superlative performances. If you are never impressed, you make even the toughest of standards seem attainable. Your athletes are led to entertain the possibility that they can achieve previously unimaginable levels of performance and are encouraged to prepare at more thorough levels.

Don't be too easily impressed. That leaves little room for improvement and fails to encourage your athletes to reach for greater heights and future excellence.

What is labeled as "good" should be ever-increasing standards of performance. What is "great" should be rarely attained.

THE COACH'S DISAPPROVAL

A Kick In The Coach's Rear

Did you ever rake an athlete over the coals in front of the entire team because he didn't do well?...Well, what if that athlete publicly took you to task because you didn't adequately prepare him for the contest? Could you hear that your preparation might not have been complete? Or would you be so focused on the threat to your authority, and the inappropriateness of both the timing and the manner of his communication, that you wouldn't hear the content? If you did hear what he said, how would his criticism of your coaching affect the way you coached? And how would it affect your relationship with him? Would it seem as though he were trying to motivate you; to help you coach better? Or, is it not his place to do so?

What if he jumped up in front of everyone and yelled at you saying that you didn't even try to coach well...You didn't care...You were always off recruiting (meeting with the board, on national team trips, at speaking engagements, whatever)...You spent all your time with the defense (the sprinters, the pitchers, the starters, the star,...take your pick)? How would you feel?...Embarrassed?...Angry?...Determined to do better?...Worthless?...Would it raise doubts about yourself?...Or, would it raise doubts about your courageous (ungrateful? recalcitrant? snotnose?) athlete?

When you think about it, if he gives you a public tongue lashing for your substandard performance, it is the same thing as your giving him one for not doing well....Oh, not exactly the same. He does not have the same power you do. You can control whether he plays. He can't control whether you coach.

And really, you are mandated with helping him play better. It may not be his place (and it certainly is not his job) to help you coach. Moreover, the consequences differ; for you, for him and for the team. He might undermine your authority, or bring into question your competence, expertise or intentions; any of which can sap your power as a coach, diminish your control over the team and have the potential to subsequently hurt the team. You must stay in authority. Decision making must remain your province. Nevertheless, the assumptions underlying a verbal reprimand of this sort, its resulting effect and its utility may be quite similar, or the same, in either case.

The Nature Of The Boot

It is difficult not to become emotionally involved with how well your athletes do. After all, you care about them. You want the best for them. And, you know that in sports the best only comes as a result of performance excellence. Furthermore, like it or not, your performance is judged on the quality of your team's play. That can be extremely frustrating. It's the epitome of a loss of control. You can't play for them, but you have a lot (often including your tenure as a coach, your salary, your professional respect, and future ability to earn a living) invested in how well they play.

When your team plays poorly, especially if you think they could have done better and you don't think they are trying, you may be tempted to get on them. After all, it is your job to motivate them. You want to get them back on track or perhaps, to stimulate them to exert more effort. And as basketball coach Jim McGregor once suggested, "A kick in the rear only serves to propel you forward and upward.". . . Right?. . . Well, maybe!

Certainly athletes often give some immediate desired response to a verbal slap on the wrist. Far too often, however, all that is elicited are apologies and promises to do better (not better behavior). Sometimes athletes will turn it around immediately following the incursion of your wrath, but is any lasting improvement made? Most often, there is not.

There are some athletes who seem to depend on a harsh word in order to put out. A kick in the butt seems to be the only thing that gets them going. And coaching folklore has it that one of the most important arts a coach can perfect is that of knowing when to pat an athlete on the back and when to kick him in the rear.

So how do we sort this all out, especially in light of the psychological research that indicates that, at least in the long run, the frequency of behavior is unchanged by verbal reprimands? Well, that is exactly what is best to do: sort it all out. As it turns out, verbal reprimands convey a number of messages, some useful, some deleterious. Let's take a close look.

Depending upon the content of the particular verbal barrage, when you let into an athlete, your kick in the rear communicates all or some of the following messages:

- Pay attention.
- That was (or, this is) important.
- That was no good.
- I know you can do better.
- You're no good.
- You're in trouble.

Some of the messages are useful. Some are not. Some athletes typically respond to the useful messages, while others tend to hear the problematic messages. Of course, most athletes will take it one way one time and another at other times, depending upon circumstances.

The Nasal 2" x 4"

Like the proverbial two-by-four across the mule's nose, your censure gets an athlete's attention. Obviously this is important.

Unless you have his attention, any attempted communication goes for naught. In fact, in many cases, getting an athlete's attention may be a critical step in motivating performance excellence, for inattention and distraction are among the most frequent impediments to performance. So occasionally (or, with some athletes, frequently), you need to do something that will command your athletes' attention.

Of course, chewing out an athlete is not the only way to get his attention. Bright lights, a whisper, firecrackers, movement, a tap on the shoulder, written notification that you wish to speak with him, Halloween masks, taking off your clothes, walking on your hands and numerous other ploys are likely to attract attention. Many of these, however, are not the best choices because of their inappropriateness, their ineffectiveness, or their undesirable consequences. Despite custom, a kick in the rear may fall among those strategies that say "pay attention," but are inappropriate and unbecoming a professional, especially since its effectiveness is questionable and its long range consequences most often undesirable.

No Laughing Matter

A boot in the rear carries the message that whatever just occurred was of significance. It may have been important for your athlete to have put forth more effort, performed the drill correctly, been where he was supposed to be on the play, listened to instructions, not misused equipment, not abused the referee or whatever. In any case, the fact that you reacted angrily to the behavior clearly communicates that the behavior in question was of considerable import—important enough to invoke your wrath. (This, of course, can be very confusing if the transgression was insignificant alone, but was the straw that broke the camel's back.)

As a coach, you are the expert on training and competitive performance. What you stress as important is valuable information. Furthermore, part of your job is to motivate your athletes. When you, the expert, stress the importance of certain behaviors, those behaviors get psychologically linked more closely with success and identified as sources for your approval or disapproval. This linkage provides considerable incentive motivation.

A kick in the rear very well may work because of the information value of its component message that says "this is important." But such information can be conveyed without resorting to anger. Of course, if you tease your athletes or kid around with them, they may not be able to discern when you are serious, really mean what you say and when something is truly important; unless you change your manner. Too many of us resort to a loud angry voice to force that distinction. Similarly, if you sometimes laugh at the same behavior for which you now get on an athlete's case, he may attribute your attack to your mood, your instability, or your misperception; rather than to the importance of his preceding action. Clearly there are better ways to communicate the message: "this is important."

Wrongo Mary-Joe!

Your disapproval clearly communicates that something is wrong, but not necessarily where it is that your team or an individual athlete has failed, let alone what would be the better or correct thing to do. This can leave your athletes at a loss as to what to do, no matter how motivated they are to do well. Furthermore, it gets them focused on their failures and your disapproval, rather than on corrective action. As a result they may begin to doubt their abilities and question your ability to help them.

Indicate what was wrong, but emphasize what they can do to do better. After all, what's already been done cannot be changed. And apologies, or promises to do better, have little value. Future excellence is what is desirable. Give them the tools and information they need to be moving in that direction.

Subpar

Often implicit in your criticism is the message: "I know you can do better." That is a tremendously valuable communication for the athlete to hear. In fact, one of the most important things a coach can do for his athletes is to raise team and individual standards and expectancies by consistently and clearly communicating that his athletes can do much better than they think they can.

"I know you can do better" is an important and integral component of a kick in the rear. If you didn't believe it were true, you probably wouldn't bother to criticize. What would be the point? Unfortunately, athletes (particularly those who react more sensitively to criticism) often have trouble picking that message out of your admonition. They get too focused on other components of the message, in particular, "You're no good" and "You're in trouble."

Communicate more directly your confidence in your athletes' ability to perform better. It is more likely to be heard that way. Moreover, such direct messages will not produce the undesirable side effects that result from communicating in anger.

The Devil To Pay

Your anger, if not punitive itself, carries with it the threat of some penalty. Implicit, at least, is the threat of loss of opportunity.

A kick in the rear carries the message: "You're in trouble." It is as if you are telling your athletes that they merit a penalty for wrongdoing.

Keep your goals in mind when chewing out your athletes. You are probably interested in providing greater incentive for learning and performance, not in exacting retribution for some "crime."

Kick The Habit

When you respond to undesirable acts with anger directed toward the performer, the kick in the rear you deliver comes as if you thought, "This athlete has done better in the past, and therefore should have done better this time. Since he did not, there is something wrong with him. He's bad." Obviously, you don't actually think those words, but a kick in the rear stems from such a belief system, even if not explicitly recognized. Why else would the criticism get conveyed in anger; and why would it be directed at the person?

You have a lot invested in your team's performance. You work hard to generate excellence. So it's frustrating when an athlete messes up, especially when you know he can do better. But your frustration better leads to action directed at fostering improvement, than to trying to change the past or seek repentance and restitution for wrongdoing.

Criticize the act, not the person. You very well may get frustrated and angry at an athlete's acts, but that's no reason to ridicule the athlete for what he has done. There's certainly no utility in doing so. Quite the contrary. It can be tremendously harmful.

There is a big difference between judging an act as to whether it is acceptable or not acceptable, good or bad, and judging a person as acceptable or not, good or bad. The athlete's performance may have been substandard or inappropriate and worthy of criticism, but the athlete never is.

When an athlete hears "you're no good" in your censure, he has two choices. He can accept your assessment; in which case, he will be invaded with self-doubts and his confidence will be impaired. Or, he can reject your implication; in which case, he rejects your judgment (and often you) in the process. Obviously, neither choice is desirable.

The Bootprint Left Behind*

As mentioned earlier, verbal reprimands usually do not effectively produce long-term change in the desired direction. In some instances, however, change does result, perhaps even in the desired direction. But even if it does, there are likely to be some undesirable side effects.

For one thing, a kick in the rear tends only to produce the desired action when in your presence. How does this encourage personal responsibility for, and pride in, a job well done?

Furthermore, you become identified as the source of personal criticism. You may tend to become aversive (scary and/or repugnant) to your athletes. As a result, they may seek to avoid you, which makes it difficult for you to help them. They may even make their sports experience one of avoidance rather than positive striving, impairing both performance and enjoyment.

As the stimulus for punishment, just the sight of you may become enough to inhibit inappropriate or substandard behavior: inhibit, not eliminate. They may change their behavior when you are around, but if the frequency of behavior remains unchanged in the long run (as the research indicates), they have to make up for lost time when you are not there or when they think you are

---

* No pun intended.

not looking. Pity the poor assistant coach who has to try to control these athletes when you are away and the behaviors that invoked your wrath are no longer suppressed.

The Missed Kick

Even when a kick in the rear apparently results in some desired change, that gain is not maintained without reinforcement. Furthermore, the boot frequently fails "to propel you forward and upward" at all.

Verbal reprimands often are not effective punishments. Your athlete may not care what you say, particularly if he has rejected your judgment, or if your disapproval has come so often as to negate its impact. Even worse, your disapproval may actually serve to maintain inappropriate behavior or poor performances with some athletes. In those cases where a chewing-out is an athlete's only source of attention from you, any recognition may be better than none. That athlete may do (often inadvertently) whatever it takes to get you to notice him.

The Bootless Shove

Fortunately, a kick in the rear is almost always accompanied by instructions for improvement. Communication of the importance of better, or different, action, and the provision of intructions often leads to movement in the desired direction. Change occurs in spite of the reprimand, however, not because of it.

Emphasis on the importance of the desired act, clear instruction for its performance, and the communication of a confidence in your athlete's ability to excel (all prior to the opportunity to act) is the best way to help him get the job done.

It is not the angry barbs that work. Instructions effectively guide behavior. Incentives motivate performance. And your communicated confidence can raise expectancy of performance excellence. Messages that indicate to the athlete that he is bad, and that he is in trouble, only elicit fear, anger, self-doubt and avoidance.

A kick in the rear may seem to propel your athletes forward and upward, but it is an illusion. Pointing your athletes in the right direction, reminding them of where they are going and letting them know they can get there works much better to push them toward their goals.

Harnessing The Propulsive Forces

You're not perfect. So, even if you strive to more directly communicate the useful component messages contained in a kick in the rear in a calm and supportive manner, once in a while you are likely to get out the old army boots and "kick butt." Even then, the results more often can be the desired increase in motivation without the undesirable side-effects if you prompt your athletes to listen for, and respond to, intent.

It pays to let your team know that if you ever chew them out, they don't need to let it get to them. They need to know that getting chewed out doesn't automatically make them feel remorseful, inadequate, threatened, angry, worthless or anything else. They control how they feel by how they choose to react, how they interpret what is said, and what they say to themselves.

Let them know that you have a common purpose and common goals. You are all in it together. Your actions, like theirs, though occasionally misdirected, are motivated by your intent to help them perform better. Help them to hear the important messages, instead of the anger. Ask them to listen for, and respond to, the messages that "You care," "You want them to do better," and "You have confidence that they can do better." Let them know a kick in the rear is only your attempt "to propel them forward and upward." And that it is their responsibility to respond to that intent and use your disapproval in a positive way.

CHAMPION MODELS

Serving Notice

When Bear Bryant first took over as head football coach at Texas A & M he is said to have "walked into a student meeting, took off his topcoat at the back of the hall, pulled off his jacket and tie as he stepped to the podium, stomped on them, then kicked them aside. Finally, he rolled up his sleeves, leaned into the microphone and announced in a low, firm voice: 'My name is Bear Bryant and I'm ready to go to work.' "[41]

Serve notice that you are serious about the pursuit of excellence and victory. Let your athletes know that you will do what it takes. Then consistently lead the way.

Model a relentless pursuit of excellence. Let your actions demonstrate that you are pleased with nothing but the best and satisfied with nothing at all, yet that you relish every second of the chase.

Joe Paterno asserts that, "A coach has to be as demanding of himself as he is of his players. He has to believe in what he is doing and then convince his players, not merely by demanding, but by instruction and example, that he is right."[42]

Monkey See, Monkey Do

It is important that you provide good models for your athletes. See to it that those individuals most likely to be modeled model desirable behaviors.

The people most likely to be emulated are you, the better athletes on the team, those individuals who have high status, those who get a lot of attention and those who are popular. Naturally, there is much overlap here. The best athletes tend to be afforded high status, enjoy considerable popularity and receive a lot of attention. Athletes who are popular with their peers tend to command a lot of attention. Athletes who enjoy high status tend to be popular. Athletes who receive a lot of attention tend to gain in status, and so on.

Consider yourself lucky if your team happens to have high-status individuals who make good peer models. But if you do not, you can do something about it. You have a tremendous amount of influence. Don't underestimate your ability to arrange for good models.

Carefully plan and control for goal-oriented peer modeling. Recruit well. Weed out the bad influences. Find out which team members are most influential among their peers. Enlist the aid of those most likely to be modeled and prompt them to play the desired role. And don't discount the effect of your actions in providing a model for your team.

Recruiting Horses To Be Aped

Recruiting is obviously one of the most important parts of coaching. As Bear Bryant used to say, "You've got to have chickens before you can make chicken salad."[43]

Recruiting is integral to virtually every coaching position, not just in college jobs. It may not be ethical, or within the rules, for example, for high school coaches to recruit athletes from another team. High school coaches are not prevented, however, from searching out their own school for the best athletes and inviting these athletes to try out for the team. Similarly, a club coach does well to go into the schools and the community to find individuals who are likely to help the team, then to actively recruit them. Baseball manager Sparky Anderson once put it this way: "The game is basically very simple. If you get good players, you win."[44]

Although obviously of major concern, athletic promise should not be a coach's sole concern in recruiting an athlete. An athlete who is going to play well, but drag the rest of the team down is no prize catch. The attitudes, training habits, and off-the-field behaviors an athlete is likely to model might be just as important in the long run as is how well the prospective recruit is likely to play.

It is not always the most talented team that wins. That's no surprise. The most talented athletes are most frequently modeled, but they do not always provide the best models.

The Sale of Hard-earned Opportunity

A good job of recruiting makes the rest of your coaching duties that much easier. The recruitment of athletes, however, can be a tricky business. Herein you are involved in the solicitation of athletes. You have to sell prospective team members on the benefits of the team. You may have to approach them. And you may have to invite them to come your way. But your program benefits the most by signing up athletes who feel privileged to have the opportunity (and are willing to invest in the right) to participate in your program and become part of the team.

Don't get lost in trying to make the sale. If you end up drooling over talented athletes or get so focused on building numbers that you put all your efforts into signing up athletes without taking care to see that new team members are enjoined properly and appreciative of the opportunity, you lose a lot of ground that can be gained by careful attention to the process. You may end up with athletes whose attitudes you don't want imitated.

Recruitment should be an information providing process. Let prospective athletes know that your program exists and the great benefits it has to offer. Clearly demonstrate that admission to your program presents a great opportunity.

Once interest is sparked, however, admission should not be made too easy. There is a lot to be said for application for admission, a tryout, an interview and probationary admission. The harder, more costly and more selective your program is perceived as being, the more your athletes will value the opportunity to play and to be part of the team and the more valued team members you will have enlisted.

Grooming The Apes

You know what behaviors you want modeled. And you usually can determine who is behaving in the desired manner, at least on the field, if not off of it. But these athletes may or may not carry any weight with their peers.

Consider yourself lucky (or a coach who has recruited successfully) if you have high status peer models who are doing the right things and doing them right. Your captains and your best athletes will be afforded considerable status. (Whether or not they maintain that status will depend on how they handle their roles.) If they are doing things well, fine. If not, it is incumbent upon you to see to it that they know the influence and responsibility that they have, they know what you want them to do and that they have incentive for acting as good role models.

It can be a different case with the athletes on your team who enjoy popularity among their peers. You may not know who they are and they may not be the models of choice. In fact, sometimes it will be their very rebelliousness that earns them status with their peers. In that case, they definitely are not the models you want to have guiding your team, unless some changes are made.

Talk to your athletes. Ask them who is popular, who has some status and who has the influence with the team. When you have identified the likely models, talk to them and make it atttractive for them to model goal-oriented behavior. You might try sitting down with the identified athlete, telling him that he is a particularly important part of the team because of his status with his peers and telling him how important it is that he lend his influence to the pursuit of team goals. Such strategy usually evokes a positive response. Athletes like to be singled out and asked for help. They often relish the responsiblity of leading. And they want to capture that championship.

Herding Out The Rotten Apples

Coaching is a helping profession. And coaches need to inspire confidence and persistence in the quest for excellence, obstacles notwithstanding. It is only with great reluctance, therefore, that coaches tend to give up on their athletes. But sometimes it must be done.

There comes a point where you've offered an athlete your help and given him his chance, but he's still hurting the team. His behavior is getting in the way of what you're trying to accomplish. Your first responsibility is to the team and, no matter how hard it might be to do, sometimes you have to let an athlete go. In fact, I often think the best investment a coach (especially a new coach) can make in the long-term good of the team, when faced with one of the better (if not the best) athletes on the team failing to get with the program, is to kick him off the team. It lets your athletes know who is in charge, that you are serious about the pursuit of excellence in your sport and that you are willing to protect the long-term interests of the team.

You hate to lose anyone, especially a good athlete. But it is worse to keep a powerful model who is leading the team astray.

Cages For Aping

One way to weed out the problems is to cut out the cancer before it spreads by giving an athlete who is causing problems his walking papers. Another way is to keep poor models separate until they get aligned with team purpose.

You might have the part of your team that is in the developmental stages of forming good habits train separately from the rest of the team. In particular, establishing an elite training group that requires the meeting of specific criteria for admittance and continuance can help foster exposure to desired peer modeling, while at the same time, providing additional incentive for excellence.

Selective Viewing

Films and videotapes are marvelous tools for modeling desired behavior. Models presented in television or film form are so effective in capturing attention that viewers learn much of what they see without requiring any special incentives to do so.

Many coaches occasionally employ films because of their emotional impact. The desirability and effectiveness of that use of video material is highly questionable. Inspirational films can enhance incentive by depicting models receiving great payoffs for superlative performances. Thus, they have some value. Films of the 1980 U.S. Olympic hockey team's gold medal winning performance are particularly well-suited to this purpose.

Of greater concern, however, is what is being taught. You must pay attention to what behavior is modeled in the films you select to show your team.

Rocky is a film often selected by coaches for their athletes' pregame viewing. It is a good film. Look at some of the desirable actions it models:

- Consistent intense training in pursuit of a clearly specified goal.
- Persistence in spite of fatigue.

- Training that pays off (Rocky performs well and reaches his goal.)
- Total commitment in training and competition.

Another advantage of *Rocky* is that once a team has seen the film, the theme song can be played during practice sessions as a symbolic reminder of the contingent relationship between diligent training and preparation and competitive success. So too, can this music be employed to stimulate feelings of confidence in your athletes when played in the competitive situation.

Rocky, however, has its drawbacks. For example, it models poor goal setting. Rocky's goal was to "go the distance," not to win. *Rocky II* models better goal setting.

Much of the benefits to be derived from viewing *Rocky* lie in its depiction of his fight preparation. As such, Rocky serves a better purpose when shown during early and mid-season, rather than just before the big game as it is most often shown.

Use films such as *Rocky*. But pay careful attention to what is modeled and use these films with a purpose in mind.

What You Give Is What You Get

Joe Paterno suggests that "A coach has to be a leader, not only by word but by example."[45] If you lose your temper, you can't expect your athletes to maintain emotional control. If your head is somewhere else when you are at practice, you can't expect your athletes to maintain their concentration. If you act as if practice is a necessary evil, the dues that must be paid in order to compete successfully, then you can't expect your athletes to be eager to train. If you exploit and deceive your athletes, you can't expect them to be honest and loyal to you. If you give up on them, you can't expect them to persist. If you don't take care of your body, how can you expect them to value taking care of theirs or, if they do, how can you expect them to respect you?

Model what you want to see. Demonstrate enthusiasm and excitement for your sport. Let your enjoyment show. Model a commitment to excellence. The attitude and behaviors your athletes exhibit are likely to appear as mirror images of those you display.

Don't monkey around. Your actions are likely to get aped.

BUILDING CONFIDENCE

Uncertain Assuredness

Confidence is something your athletes either have or do not have, and you sure as heck hope they have it when they need it. Right?...Wrong! Confidence consists of feelings, thoughts, and behaviors whose occurences can be preprogrammed, practiced and intentionally generated.

Confidence comes with good goals, good preparation, familiarity with success, predictions of success, reexperiencing past success and giving the appearance of assuredness. Build a confident team. Don't wait (and hope) for it to happen.

Freeing The Magician

Earlier I suggested that it pays to believe that your team can excel. You must be open to the idea that there are no limits to how far your team can go.

There is nothing magical about believing that your team has no limits. Such a belief does not ensure success. It will allow you, however, to work what magic you do have. It will dissolve many artificial barriers that otherwise might block your progress, and it will encourage you to do what it takes to excel.

Furthermore, your unmitigated belief in your team's prospects will build your athletes' confidence. If your belief consistently shows, theirs will follow.

Football coach Duffy Daugherty suggests that, "Every coach worth his practice cap must believe in himself and he must believe in his players...and he must be able to communicate this belief in his players...and he must be able to communicate this belief in his coaching."[46]

Sometimes They Have To Read It In The Papers

Affirm your athletes' abilities. Repeatedly let them know that they can and will do it.

Utilize all available resources to convey your message to them. Tell them with everything you say and do. Let them hear you tell others. And let them hear you tell the media.

Following the Boston Celtic Game 1 1985 NBA Championship Series romp of his Los Angeles Lakers, coach Pat Riley told reporters, "I have never seen a team, except ours at times, shoot from the perimeter like that."

What a clear vote of confidence delivered through the media from a coach to his team. The Lakers had just been blown out, and here their coach was telling the world what a marvelous performance they had just seen by the opposition. The opposition had performed better than any team he had ever seen, *except ours at times.*" The message was clear: the only team to ever play that well before is ours, and it is not unusual for us. We can easily turn it around. . . . The Lakers won the championship.

Expectations Of Excellence

Sherm Chavoor, who coached Mark Spitz, reports, "I drive 'em to give me more than they think they have in them."[47] That is one of the keys to coaching excellence: clearly communicating to your athletes that they can perform much better than they ever before had imagined was possible.

What you ask of your athletes is critical. You must expect excellence in order to get it. Ask for it. And accept nothing less.

Matter-of-fact Excellence

A coach must clearly communicate, in every way possible, that he knows his athletes can do better than they think they can. Tell them they can do it. Give them opportunities to do things they don't think they can do, but present these challenges in a manner that says, "Of course you can do it."

The way in which you present a challenge communicates a lot. A matter-of-fact presentation of an extremely difficult challenge lets your athletes know that you think they can do it. If your presentation says, "This is hard. Most of you can't do it, but try anyway," then most of the team will "try," but not succeed. Either way, you're the expert. If you let them know they can, they'll probably believe that they can. If you show some doubt, they will think you are asking them to do something unrealistic.

Repeated Opportunity

Plant the seeds of confidence and excellence. Provide formidable challenges. Refuse to accept failure. And furnish repeated opportunity for success. Identify some desirable standard of excellence and encourage your team to persist until they meet that specified criterion.

Give them a challenge. If they fail to meet it, give them another opportunity.

Again, how you tell your team to stick with it until they get it makes a big difference. You don't want to make them repeat a drill as punishment ("We're going to stay here and repeat this until you get it right.")

Approach it in a different manner. ("That's not it. It's got to be better. Let's do it again.") Give them an additional opportunity to meet the challenge. This kind of approach says both, "high standards are important," and "I know you want to, can, and will make the grade."

Disconfirming Doubts

Even if you do an excellent job of presenting formidable challenges to your athletes in a way that subtly, but clearly, communicates that they can do it, they sometimes won't believe you. They still will have their doubts. Then you need to show them that they can. When talk isn't enough, you have to hit them over the head with experience. The most effective way to destroy the beliefs about their abilities (or lack thereof) that limit their performances is to arrange for experiences that disconfirm their doubts.

Late in the 1981 collegiate swimming season University of Texas All American swimmer William Paulus was swimming poorly and starting to worry about it. One day toward the end of practice, William was bemoaning the way he felt in the water. Texas coach Eddie Reese told William to get up on the starting block and swim a 50 yd. butterfly for time. William balked at tackling the swim. He had little confidence in his ability to go a fast one. Eddie insisted that William do it and told him in a matter-of-fact manner that he did not want him to go any faster than 22.7 sec. for the swim.

Now, 22.7 is a very fast time for a 50 yd. butterfly practice swim. But when Eddie told William that he "didn't want him to go any faster than 22.7," he presented it in a way that suggested to William that William could swim much faster than that, if only Ed would let him. William went a 22.4. A few weeks later he broke the world record for the 100 meter butterfly.

The Rich Get Richer

In order to improve, your athletes must constantly accept demanding challenges. But if the challenge is too tough or too easy, motivation wanes. Finding a challenge that presents the right probability of success is critical.

Your athletes need to believe that they have a chance to succeed, but only with excellent performances. If success is a relatively sure thing, motivation is likely to be low. Furthermore, this somewhat meaningless success is likely to do little or nothing to enhance confidence. If success is thought to be out of reach, the motivation to try may be low. Even worse, the imminent failure that follows from a token effort reinforces self-doubt and increases future fear of failure.

In general, it works well to present your athletes with challenges that they are likely to successfully handle about 50% of the time. Those of your athletes who have had a history of failure may be more reluctant to tackle a challenge with only a 50-50 chance of success and may be more pessimistic about the likelihood of success when they do. It is usually better, therefore, to give these athletes challenges that present a greater probability of success. Athletes with a history of more frequent success will be more likely to eagerly and confidently tackle challenges where the perceived probability of success is lower. As a resulting paradox, you might have to present challenges that represent smaller incremental improvements in performance to the very athletes in most need of large improvement.

The Confident Helmsman

Success breeds confidence. This doesn't mean that you should set it up so that your athletes are faced with challenges that they can always handle (in other words, no challenges at all). They do not have to succeed every time. In fact, confidence is enhanced more by the successful accomplishment of a challenge that was previously lost, than by a perfect record over insignificant foes.

Failure need not be devastating. It's not important that your athletes always remain on course, only that when they stray they make the necessary correction. It's the experience of getting back on course that insulates your athletes from doubt and gives them confidence that they can make it to their destination.

Looking Cocky At All Times

Part of having a confident team is getting your athletes to look the part. Notre Dame quarterback Frank Carideo reports that Knute Rockne emphasized to all of his quarterbacks the importance of radiating confidence. "Rock would say: 'I want you cocky at all times. *At all times*! Without letup. For several reasons. First of all, it shows the other team that you have complete confidence and you know exactly what you're going to do next. There's no doubt in your mind.' He even wanted us to be mindful of our facial expressions, so we could indicate we not only knew what we were going to do but that we were going to pull it off successfully no matter how they try to stop us."[48]

Appearing confident not only effects the opposition's expectancies about the impending outcome of the contest, but it also helps your team to feel confident. As they act the part, they begin to truly experience the role. And their opponents will help them. The other teams often will act with deference to a confident looking team, thereby giving your team additional cause for feeling confident.

CHAMPIONSHIP PREPARATION

What If Your Star's Shoelaces Come Untied?

The majority of practice time should be devoted to preparation for doing well in competition. Part of that preparation, however, is to prepare to handle the things that go wrong.

Anticipate undesirable events that may occur so that you can have your athletes practice coping with them. Anticipate everything that you can possibly think of that might go wrong — bad weather, poor calls by the referees, bad bounces, injuries to key players, disqualifications, outstanding performances by the opposition, faulty equipment, poor performances by your key players, getting behind when you expected to be ahead and so forth. You want to be ready to handle everything you can think of that might occur.

A good place to start is to take inventory of unexpected events that influenced past contests. Identify the things that came up in the past that you would have liked to have better prepared your team to handle. And take examples from the times that you won because your opponents failed to handle unexpected events.

The little things count. Account for every last detail. Joe Paterno suggests, "A coach has to have a plan for everything. For when he's ahead, for when he's behind and when he's tied, for what he's going to say to his squad and to the press after the game."[49]

One of Bear Bryant's favorite expressions was, "It's the itty-bitty, teeny-tiny things that beat you." He was said to rehearse problems that might arise in a game over and over again. So diligent was the Bear in his preparation for even the unlikeliest of contingencies that he was said to have had " 'a game plan for a hurricane in the first quarter, a flood in the second, a drought in the third, and an eagle swooping down to block a field goal in the fourth. ' " When asked about the tale, Bryant reportedly chuckled, but didn't deny it. 'Well,' he said, 'we do try to be prepared.' "[50]

Former U.C.L.A. basketball star (and coach at his alma mater) Larry Farmer says, "Coach [John] Wooden had one time period devoted to how to tie our shoelaces so they would never slip."[51]

But what if they did?* Would your athletes be prepared?

After The Fall

Your team is always better prepared if you have anticipated as many undesirable events as possible and have had your athletes practice coping with them. Notice I said that you should try to "anticipate" the undesirable events and have your athletes practice "coping" with them. You don't want to spend a lot of time thinking about or discussing the things that might go wrong. Neither do you want your athletes to devote a lot of attention to them. The more you (and your athletes) think about ways for things to go wrong, the more you are practicing and getting good at having them go wrong.

On the other hand, you can identify things that might go wrong and prepare to handle them without practicing to make things go wrong if you take them from after the fact.

Start at the point where some identified thing already has gone wrong. Then any discussion and practice of coping

---

* Even the most accomplished of athletes occasionally have things like this happen. He had an incredible string of 81 straight victories, when Edwin Moses' shoelaces came untied in the finals of the 1983 World Track and Field Championships. This champion coped and kept his string of victories alive.

strategies does not have to include a rehearsal (even imagined) of the undesired event. This way the events become signals for your athletes to plug in prepared coping strategies, without having practiced the very things you wish to have them avoid.

Expect The Unexpected

You want to anticipate every conceivable contingency and prepare your team to handle it. Part of such preparation is preparing them for the unexpected.

No matter how thoroughly you prepare your team for the contest, you will not be able to anticipate everything that will happen. Things are likely not to go exactly according to plan. Teach your athletes flexibility even for the high pressure situation. And help them to understand that as valuable as it is to have your game plan so well rehearsed that it will plug in automatically as planned, things do not need to go perfectly in order for the team to perform superlatively. Your athletes must cope, however, with whatever comes up.

Planned Familiarity

Acclimate your athletes to the conditions under which they are likely to perform. If there is any possible way you can have your team compete at the site of your championship, do it for the experience. If not, at least scout it out.

It helps for your athletes to know where everything is, to know what the procedures will be and to be ready for everything. If you cannot take them to the site in advance, show them films, video tapes, or still pictures of other competitions in that arena. Play sound recordings of previous events. Descriptions of where everything is, customary procedures and what to expect are helpful.

Have your athletes visualize what it will be like to compete at that particular site amidst the hustle and bustle of the crowd and their competition. Have them use the information you gave them to set the stage for imaginally practicing *their winning performances* within the context in which they are to take place.

If possible, a dress rehearsal is near ideal. Having done it before only makes it that much easier to do it again. Mike Brown, University of Texas and Longhorn Diving Club coach, used this advice to have his divers experience the 1980 Olympic Diving Trials prior to the actual event. They rehearsed the entire meet, complete with judges, spectators and appropriate competition times. (Of course, it helped that the Swim Center at the University of Texas was the site for the 1980 Olympic Diving Trials. Nevertheless, you can prepare your athletes to feel right at home by structuring a rehearsal that duplicates anticipated conditions as nearly as possible.) Brian Bungham even rehearsed the experience of diving immediately following an imaginary Greg Louganis dive that was awarded 10s (definitely a tough act to follow; and, as it turns out, he did have to follow it). Brian, who made the U.S. Olympic Team along with teammates Mark Virts and Cynthia Potter, came up from an early-round, high scoring-dive in the Trials, smiled, and commented to Mike, "This is great! It's just like practice."

"The Itty-bitty, Teeny-tiny Things"

At the moment of truth, you not only want to be optimally prepared, you want to look ready. Serve notice on the competition that nothing was omitted in your preparation.

Prior to every game, Bear Bryant reportedly led "his team in a streetclothes tour of the stadium before retiring to the locker room. Following their coach's example, the players peer at the sun, test the wind, check the footing on the field. The message to rivals is clear: Alabama is checking things out. Alabama will be ready."[52]

THE LOW PRESSURE CHAMPIONSHIP

Stressing The Problem

Conditions do not have to be ideal in order for a team to perform superlatively, but the closer to ideal, the better. Detailed planning helps. You want your athletes to be healthy, rested, well-conditioned, practiced, confident, eligible and ready to go.

Part of optimal readiness should include freedom from excess stress. Undue stress can interfere with performance. Doubts, uncertainties, worries and fears all distract and tighten-up your athletes, waste energy and impair performance.

Athletes experiencing stress will tend to be overburdened with Self, instead of concentrating on the game. They tend to observe the symptoms of nervousness and worry about them. They observe and evaluate themselves as they go. They tend to focus on how well they are doing, rather than on what they are doing. As a result, they tend to be more susceptible to being sucked into playing their opponent's game, rather than sticking to their own game plan.

Athletes experiencing stress tend to be overwhelmed with negative thoughts. They tend to focus on failure and catastrophize about (real, imagined, and mostly unspecified) consequences of poor performances. They tend to imagine the very performances they wish to avoid, imaginally rehearsing them in the process. They tend to entertain thoughts of inadequacy, which tend to serve as self-fulfilling prophecies.

At best such stress is discomforting and distracting. At worst, it can be devastating to performance.

It is unlikely that you will be able to eliminate all stress reactions in your athletes. Sporting events have become too socially valued and too highly visible, and athletes have had to make too large a commitment to their sport, for it to be taken lightly. With proper planning, however, you can go a long way to reduce the amount of stress your athletes will experience in competition. And you can help prepare your athletes to perform extremely well in spite of any stress they might experience.

Taking Care Of Unfinished Business

How often are your athletes in attendance at a game or practice, but not there at all? Their heads are off somewhere else.

Unfinished business can be tremendously distracting and stress-producing. If an athlete isn't there, you need to get his head into the game...or, send him home.

Of course ideally, all outside worries and cares are taken care of prior to arrival at the sports arena, or at least they are put aside before practice or the game begins. Nevertheless, there will be many times when your athletes haven't taken care of business and are preoccupied with something unfinished in their lives.

Once you have assessed that some unfinished business is the problem, ask them if there is any action that can be taken to alleviate the problem. If not, this fact must be recognized and the athlete must come to grips with it. Resignation that life doesn't always go as desired, and that nothing can be done about it, is sometimes enough to allow an athlete to put aside his personal problems and to concentrate on his sport. When it is not, it often is because he ends up ruminating about some perceived catastrophic consequences he feels are likely to result from the problem. In that case, he should be prompted to explore the following questions:
- "What's the worst that can happen?"
- "What are the odds that the worst will actually happen?"
- "If the worst does happen, how bad would the worst actually be?"

Answers to these questions usually put things in their proper perspective and remove much of the perceived threat.

If there is something that can be done to take care of the athlete's unfinished business, you should ask him if he is clear on what it is he can do and when he can do it. Such questioning forces the athlete to approach the problem in a goal-oriented fashion, rather than being distracted and burdened with ruminating about some imagined awful consequences. The knowledge that he has devised a plan of action and has scheduled a specific time to take care of the problem should remove much of the burden and allow him to concentrate on what he is doing.

Most of the time there will be nothing the athlete can do until later to take care of whatever is bothering him. Even if he could do something about the problem right then, he often could just as easily take care of it at a later time. If he makes an appointment with himself to take care of business at an appropriately scheduled time, he knows he is on the way to resolution of his problem.

If whatever must be done is vitally important, and must be done at the present time or not at all, the athlete probably ought to be sent to take care of his business. He wasn't contributing anyway (remember, that's where we started). Perhaps he can take care of his unfinished business and make a contribution (to himself and the team) when he returns.

Academic Planning

Academic work will be a major factor in the lives of athletes who attend junior high school, high school, college or graduate school. A significant amount of their time will be spent daily in school. And they are likely to be faced with substantial academic demands. When they have papers due, tests coming up, homework piling up or projects hanging over their heads, they will likely experience stress.

Whether or not an athlete is academically interested or inclined, academic demands are a potential (and likely) source of stress. Advance planning can take a lot of pressure off your athletes.

Encourage your students to get ahead in their work. This is usually perceived as a weird or unusual idea, but as Bell (1982) points out "winning isn't normal," it requires extraordinary acts.[53] Students are permitted to lighten their workload by beginning their reading, homework assignments, papers and the like prior to the start of the semester or the school year. They need only to explain their intentions to their instructors and request the assignments in advance. If they find out when they are going to have tests, what reading assignments are going to be due and when, what papers and projects are going to be due and when, then they can plan to meet these responsibilities and get a jump on doing so.

Of particular concern are tests and papers that are going to be due at approximately the same time as league, state or national championship tournaments. You don't want your athletes worried about papers or tests when they need to be concentrating on the big game. (This is in no way intended to discount the importance of academic work or to attribute higher priority to sports. It is merely intended to suggest that both can be taken care of, and conflicts between the two minimized, with proper organization and planning.)

If athletes are going to have papers due at a time that will conflict with a game, suggest that they turn them in early, instead of requesting permission to turn them in late. The same goes for tests. Suggest athletes seek permission to take tests in advance of an away game, rather than having to take a make-up exam upon their return. Such academic preparation will free your athletes from a lot of undue academic stress.

"My Okapi Is Missing!"

Even minor irritations can become tremendously stressful in the context of a championship situation. The wise coach heads off as many potential disturbances as possible.

Encourage your athletes to make sure they take to the championships everything they need and think they might want. They don't have to pack way in advance, but they should be encouraged to make a list of what they will pack and to keep the list handy so that they might add to it as they think of things they might have forgotten.

Equipment usually can be replaced. But why have them use equipment that they are not used to or that has yet to be broken-in, if advance planning can prevent the change? You want them to be as comfortable with their surroundings as possible. Their own equipment helps. So too does it help to take along broken-in spares.

Similarly, you don't want an athlete going bananas because she forgot her pet stuffed okapi, her lucky hat or her toothbrush. Athletes have been known to come unglued at a championship for less important things than forgetting something like a toothbrush that can be replaced anywhere. Peak performance can be fragile.

Coach, Not Counselor

An athlete's personal relationships can be great sources of support and encouragement. Unfortunately, they also can be sources of tremendous stress and distraction.

Many an athlete has let a season's training and preparation slip away from him because he was so upset about a conflict with parents or a girlfriend that he couldn't perform. And many a team has let some interpersonal conflict between two team members escalate until it divided the team into two warring factions.

Resolving personal conflicts may not necessarily be a coach's province. In fact, although athletes tend to seek out their coaches to vent interpersonal concerns, most coaches are not trained to do counseling or therapy. Instead of assuming a burden they are not adequately prepared to handle, coaches should refer their athletes to trained professionals.

It is a coach's province, however, to remind his athletes to take care of their personal business before it interferes with the team. Remind your athletes that come the time of the championship they want to be free to focus on their sport and to have as smooth sailing as possible. Relationship problems can interfere with that freedom. Recommend that if they are concerned about a relationship, they deal with the problem well in advance of the championship. This is particularly important if there are any hard feelings or conflicts weighing heavily on their relationships with teammates, coaches, parents or anyone else with whom an encounter at the championships is likely to be upsetting or distracting. Remind your athletes that they don't have to like each other; they merely need to accept each other, encourage each other, support each other and play well together.

Nothing To Lose

Much of the debilitating stress experienced by athletes comes as a result of the "what ifs." "What if I don't do well?" "What if I'm not ready?" "What if I blow my big chance?" "What if I lose?"

Well, what if?...So what? There is nothing to lose. That's one of the nice things about sports. There is absolutely nothing to lose. There are lots of rewards that accrue with victory, but no punishment delivered for defeat. There are no fines assessed the loser. No one gets flogged for losing. (At least there are no provisions for flogging the loser structured into a sporting event.) When an athlete does poorly, no punishment is exacted. No aversive event is introduced and no prize possession is taken away. There is no loss exacted at all.

Take the pressure off of your athletes. Help them see that there is no danger in defeat.

Eying Victory vs. Shying From Defeat

There is no danger in defeat. There is nothing to lose. This by no means makes victory any less desirable, or defeat any more palatable. The object of any sport always is victory.

There is a fine distinction here — one that a coach should help his athletes make. *Winning must be of paramount importance, but defeat is inconsequential.*

Victory must be the focus of attention in pursuit. To dwell on defeat is to needlessly invite stress and promote poor performance. The incentive should come from the potential spoils of victory, not from avoiding the imagined perils of defeat.

For that matter, it is actually the quest for victory that makes sports so exciting, *the quest, not the conquest.* The consequences, while sometimes substantially materially rewarding, are not earth-shattering, whether in victory or defeat. As Winston Churchill once said, "Success is never final, failure is never fatal."

What If You're Not Home When Michael Anthony Calls?

When athletes fail in their pursuit of victory, no ills befall them. They merely miss opportunities to reap the rewards that await the victors.

There's a big difference between a missed opportunity and a penalty. Not getting something good is not the same as getting something bad.

I often point out to athletes that I would have loved it if someone had knocked on my door this morning and handed me a cashier's check for one million dollars. But, now that I have conjured up the possiblity of that good fortune befalling me and recognized that this morning had passed without such an occurence, it makes no sense for me to upset myself that I am not now a millionaire. I have taken no losses.

Victory and performance excellence hold many rewards. They are worth pursuing. But poor performance and defeat hold no penalty. They are not worth fearing.

When your athletes get worried about the prospect of defeat, let them know that losing warrants no attention. Deflate their concern. Ask them "What's the worst that can happen?" "How bad would that be anyway?" and "What are the odds of the worst coming about?" Help them discover that a missed opportunity could be disappointing, but the prospect need not be threatening. Reasoning it out, in this case, is a lesson much preferable to that provided by experience.

The Burden Of Ego

Work with your athletes to get them to rate their performances without judging their *Selves*. It is imperative that they have some criteria against which they measure their performances. That's the only way they can improve and excel. And goals do a lot to create excitement, add meaning and maintain interest in sports. But such standards provide means of measuring performance, not personal worth.

If your athletes put their egos on the line when they compete, they're bound to find competition psychologically stressful. It need not be. It can be an exciting opportunity to see how well they can do. *The contest should never be viewed as a test of how good they are.*

Encourage them to take pride in their successes, to feel good about what they did. But don't challenge their worth. Don't present the game as a chance to see "what they are made of."

Allow them to be disappointed with their failures, but not disappointed with themselves. *Criticize the act, not the person*.

There is a big difference between failing and being a failure. Help your athletes make the distinction. They need to be free to fail, if they are going to be unencumbered in their quest to excel.

Ten Of The Many Ways To Avoid Losing

Since, as pressure mounts, there is such a tendency to avoid losing, I thought I might present you with some sure-fire, and not-so-sure-fire, ways to avoid losing. You, in turn, might want to pass them on to your athletes.

- **Don't play**. Clearly the surest-fire way to avoid defeat.
- **Don't try**. If you don't try, you might not win. But you can always say you would have won if you had tried.
- **Wreck the game**. If you totally wreck the game there can be no winner, but you can't lose. Even if you don't succeed in totally wrecking the game, but at least succeed in taking away the value of the contest, people will be less likely to notice whether you won or lost; and if by chance they do notice, they probably won't care.
- **Create problems**. This is one way to wreck the game. If you create enough of a problem, someone might stop the game. At the very least, if you are enough of a problem, then you will be removed from the game. If you are not playing, you can't lose. And, as a bonus, you get to say that you would have won if you had been permitted to stay in the game.
- **Don't play the entire game**. If you never play the whole game, you can always say you would have won if you had

played. And if you are real lucky, the game will never get completed. Then you can't lose.

- **Prearrange to have an excuse**. If you miss practice, get sick, lose your equipment or set up some other unsurmountable obstacle; no one can expect you to win, blame you for losing or think less of you when you do.
- **De-emphasize the contest**. If this particular game doesn't really count, then neither does losing it. You're safe. If you don't care about this one, you can't really lose; because if you cared, you would have prepared differently, tried harder, and surely won.
- **Keep others from winning**. The least you can do is keep others around you from winning. In that way, if you don't win, you won't look so bad in contrast. Drag others down. Put others down. Keep others down. Do all you can to prevent them from winning.
- **Play the nice guy**. If you are nice enough no one will tell anyone (including you) that you lost. Then you never have to deal with it.
- **Win.**

Which strategy should you teach your team to go for?

You Can Take It Lying Down

Relaxation training should be an important part of every coach's program. Relaxation skills are easily taught, easily acquired (especially for athletes) and joyfully experienced (besides proving extremely valuable, relaxation just plain feels good).

There are many benefits to be derived from teaching relaxation skills to your team. Among the benefits are their use for minimizing and handling stress in the competitive situation. Athletes can be taught to use relaxation skills to generate a cool, calm and collected approach to the championships. And they can be taught to plug in relaxation to combat the symptoms of the stress reaction, lowering arousal when it occurs.

Relaxation training can be done as a formal part of your training program, but it doesn't have to be handled this way. You can let your athletes learn it on their own, utilizing commercially available audio tapes. Either way, relaxation training need not take up much time. Athletes can become extremely proficient in its use with only two or three twenty minute training sessions per week for two or three weeks and then a few minutes practice a day from then on. It pays great returns for a minimal investment of time pleasantly spent. . . . Sometimes your team can improve while lying down on the job.

A Clairvoyant Misses The Suspense

As the big game draws near, athletes tend to check frantically for signs that they will do well. They are chronically turning inward for a microscopic inside look at how they feel, searching for indicators that they are moving toward that moment of peak readiness when they will be "in the groove."* And they look to every conceivable outside source for assurances, centering their efforts on trying to get reassured by their coach. They want to *know* that their training will payoff, that they *are* going to do well.

You cannot honestly assure them that they will do well. All you can do is tell them the truth – that there is no way to know how well they will do until they play, that they do not need to know in advance that they are going to do well in order to do well, and that feeling assured will not necessarily ensure good performances.

---

* not realizing that that peak state only occurs when they stop consciously searching for and evaluating the signs the body provides, and instead get so absorbed in what they are doing that they are in "the flow," passively reading the cues that their environment (internal and external) sends and actively responding in a goal-striving manner.

Ask them what reason they have to believe that they cannot do well without knowing that they will, or in spite of having doubts. Let them know that they can feel confident. Tell them that you think they can do well, and are likely to do so, because they have prepared well (assuming, of course, that they have prepared well).

Remind them that the fact of the matter is that they cannot possibly know anyway whether or not they will do well, until such time that they either do or do not. Ask them what benefits they derive from spending a lot of time and energy needlessly worrying themselves in search of an answer they cannot possibly find.

And, perhaps most importantly of all, suggest to them that it is the very uncertainty as to the outcome that makes the sporting contest as exciting as it is.

The Giraffe Provides No Assurances

How do you know whether your team is ready and will do well?...You don't!

I mention the obvious because it is not only athletes who worry themselves out of good performances trying to find certainty in the impending outcome. Coaches have been known to fatigue or injure their athletes in last minute drills that are directed more at allaying the coach's uncertainty than at more thorough preparation for the contest.

You can't know in advance how well your team is going to do. Since you cannot, it makes little sense to try to reassure yourself of their impending success with drills or scrimages designed to see if your team is ready. Too many coaches leave the game on the practice field that way. It's foolish. It's like digging up potatoes to see how they are growing.

We used to have a growth chart hanging in my daughters' room. It was a poster of a giraffe (with lines indicating inches from the floor) in front of which we used to stand my daughters and record their heights by taking a pencil, placing it on top of their heads, and making a mark on the calibrated chart. One day my older daughter, Kirsten (who was two at the time), came running into the living room all excited. "Daddy, I just measured myself," she declared. "You did!" I complimented. Then I inquired, "How tall are you?" She placed her hand flat on the top of her head and proudly announced, "This tall!". . . Well, Kirsten was exactly right. That's how tall she was. I think it was about then that we stopped using the chart to watch her growth.

Your team will do as well as it does. They will be as ready as they are come time for the contest. All you can do is prepare them the best you possibly can. And there is no way of knowing in advance how well they will do. Don't interfere with their optimal preparation in an abortive attempt to find out.

The Competitive Get-together

There may be times when you will need to stress the importance of a competition to your athletes. For the big games, the big meets or the major tournaments, however, that rarely is necessary. Your athletes know how important the big contest is, and (although the outcome may not impact their livelihood as it can yours) they want it badly. In fact, most of the time it will pay for you to put things back in perspective for them. Often the major competitions seem to take on such importance that athletes act as if a win will make their life, and as if a loss has life-threatening consequences. They create so much undue stress that they cannot perform optimally in the most important sports event of their lives.

Immediately prior to their 1981 NCAA team championship victory in their home pool, I tried to help put things in perspective for the University of Texas swimming team. I told them that they thought they were vying for the NCAA Championships. "The NCAA Championships! Now that sounds like some heavy duty deal. It can seem pretty scary."

"The truth is," I suggested, "the NCAA has sent out invitations to all of its member institutions, inviting them to send any of their athletes, who have met the qualifying standards, here to our little swimming hole for a get-together to see who can go up and down the pool the fastest."

"That's all it is, all any swimming meet is: a bunch of guys getting together to see who can go up and down the pool the fastest. Now that's not scary. It's fun. It's fun to race. What's the first thing you do when you get into the water with a friend? 'Hey! I'll race you to the ladder.' And you want a challenge. So, if your friend isn't a competitive swimmer of your caliber, it's, 'I'll give you a head start,' or 'You swim freestyle, I'll swim butterfly.' This meet can be the most fun. The swimmers who can give you the best races are all gathered here at the same time to see who can go up and down the pool the fastest. That's exciting!"

POSITIVE STRIVING

Positive Striving

Your athletes will perform much better if they are actively striving to reach their goals and win, rather than working to avoid losing and performing poorly. Avoidance motivation only gets your athletes focused on the very things they do not want to do and on results that are viewed as if they have awful consequences. It gets them playing tight, with fear, and distracted; all of which interferes with performance and takes away considerably from the fun. Positive striving, on the other hand, enhances concentration, gets athletes playing loose, eagerly pursuing victory and enjoying the quest for victory. When they want to win, instead of playing to avoid losing, they play better and have more fun.

Joe Paterno encourages such an approach. "I tell our kids never to be afraid to lose. Think about winning. I don't want anybody playing for me who is afraid when he walks out on that football field that he's going to make a mistake that will cost us a football game."[54] He says, "We tell our players, 'Don't worry about losing. Just relax and do your best. Enjoy it.' "[55]

Limiting Opportunity

A major university track coach requested my advice on a problem he was having. It seemed that some of his athletes were trying to get out of going to some of the school's scheduled track meets. In the past he had required participation in all the meets. Now, he was considering making them go to only ten of their twelve scheduled meets and letting each athlete select the two he wanted to skip. He wanted to know if I thought it would be better to require that team members go to all the meets or to let them select two they did not want to attend.

My answer was, "neither." Why build avoidance habits? He was already pretty unhappy about his athletes wishing to avoid competition. He wanted them to be chomping at the bit to get to compete. So I suggested that he make "getting to compete" a privilege by not "allowing" team members to go to any more than ten of the team's twelve scheduled meets. Then, instead of letting them choose which meets they wanted to miss, he could let them select the ten meets in which they desired most to be allowed to participate. By presenting competition as something that athletes could choose, rather than as something they could reject, and by limiting an athlete's opportunity to compete, he could show competition in a much more attractive light.

After The Thrill Is Gone

Success breeds confidence. It can also make winning that much more difficult. As former UCLA coach John Wooden says, "The more you win, the harder it is to keep doing it."[56]

The more you win, the more everyone else comes gunning for you. The prospect of victory over your team provides greater incentive. So while some teams will expect you to win and will roll over and concede victory before the game begins, most teams, especially the better ones, will prepare better and exert more effort in an attempt to pull off an upset victory.

The far greater challenge, however, lies within your own team. As victory becomes more commonplace, it can become less rewarding. It can become like an old hat – comfortable and hardly noticed. Meanwhile the pressures to defend your title can be great. So great, that the tendency is to start focusing on exactly that ("defending the title"), instead of focusing on *capturing* the title again. Your team may get to where, as the song says, "You don't care about winning, but you don't want to lose." This avoidance motivation gets your team looking in the wrong direction, feeling the stress, and wanting to get safely through the championship and "get it over with;" rather than eagerly anticipating "getting into it," as positive striving would lead them to do. Even worse, even if they do manage to overcome the stress and the focus on "avoiding losing," and they do win, victory may not seem that big of a deal. It may be perceived only as what they were "supposed to do." Then there is no thrill of victory, merely the "relief" of not losing.

Take some pressure off your athletes by giving them the facts. Let them know that despite what the press and the program might say, this team is not the defending champion. This year's team might be comprised of some members of last year's championship team, but it also has some new personnel. The team is different. The chemistry is different. The circumstances are different. Though many of the athletes on the team may have been on last year's championship team, this particular *team* has never won a championship. Now, they have that opportunity. And with the skill and experience of the returning veterans, they have an excellent chance to *capture* a championship for themselves.

THE PREGAME SHOW

Remember The Alamo

Your pregame talk to your athletes should have a clear purpose and well-designed plan for achieving that purpose. It is not enough to give them a fire and brimstone speech designed to get them tearing down the lockers. Nor is it necessarily desirable. In fact, it is highly doubtful that it pays to get your team at all physiologically aroused for the game. As football coach Ron Meyer said, "I'll take execution any day over emotion. There was great emotion at the Alamo, and there weren't any survivors there."

Worming Your Way Into Victory

Often before the big game your team will already "want it plenty badly." You don't need to get them "up." You may need, however, to loosen them up. A joke will often do well. A joke that contains some pertinent messages, and well-timed modeling can work even better.

Almost legendary is the performance Baylor football coach Grant Teaff gave his team prior to a major upset of a formidable Texas team. He stepped out of role with an outrageous act that both modeled a willingness to do whatever it might take to win and invited his team to step out of the role of underdog. It emphasized the importance of the contest, but in a tone that clearly signified that the game's outcome would not be the end of the world.

Coach Teaff told his team a story of two Eskimos ice fishing. One caught fish after fish, while the other never got a bite. Finally the unsuccessful Eskimo asked the other what he was doing differently that he was having so much success. "Easy," the successful fisherman replied, "I keep the worms warm in my mouth." At that point Teaff exclaimed that he would do whatever it took to succeed, pulled a worm out of his pocket, and dropped it in his mouth. . . . As already mentioned, Baylor won.

Say It With Purpose

Pregame talks are best approached purposefully with some clearly defined goals and a specific plan of action that includes modeling the desired approach to the game. Pep talks aren't all they are cut out to be. Usually their value lies in their emphasis on the importance of the contest (which the team should already know) and the message that they provide that says, "I know you can do it." (Why else would you be ranting and raving like you are?)

If your purpose is to remind your team of the importance of victory, you may be doing more harm than good. Winning is clearly the goal of any sport. It never should be discounted. But, most of the time, your team is already acutely aware of that fact. When you remind them, you only run the risk of heightening the anxiety of an already anxious group. If you need to ventilate some of your anxiety, your pregame talk is not the place to do it. As basketball coach Abe Lemons suggests, "A lot of time you get too high for a team. The way I look at all basketball games, you've got to keep your players level-headed. All that hurrah and getting up for it will not do that much good. A lot of times teams just want it too bad."

Your pregame talk is, however, a good place to provide a few last minute instructions, a reminder of key things on which to focus, and adjustments to the specific situation and conditions that you face. In other words, it should be task-oriented. As coach Lemons puts it, "You've got to go in like it's a job." (Albeit, a tremendously fun and exciting job.)

A pregame talk also is a good place to demonstrate your willingness to pull out all stops and go the extra yard (à la Grant Teaff). Let your team know that "a little extra" is what it is going to take to win, you're going to do it, and you expect they also will want to.

In your pregame talk you might do well to downplay the consequences of defeat. They pose no threat. Most of all, it pays to emphasize the fun and excitement of the challenge that lies before you. More often than not, the best thing you can do is to end your pregame talk with a reminder to "have fun!"

A Time And A Place

I have suggested that your pregame talk might include a few last minute instructions, . . . but only a few. They should be minimized. There is a time for learning, and a time for performance. Whenever possible, these periods should be separated.

Last minute instructions also shouldn't be too detailed. They should include mention of the relevant goal and a description of the best route for getting there, not step-by-step directions. Too detailed an analysis can hinder performance. Contest time is the time to turn them loose and let them play.

Going To The Source

Athletes differ considerably as to their preferences regarding precompetitive activities. Some athletes want to be left alone immediately prior to entering the competition so that they might have some uninterrupted time to get their heads straight. They may want to imaginally rehearse some key components of their desired performance; or they may want to relax in order to conserve energy, stay calm and enhance their power of concentration. Other athletes prefer some diversion that will distract them from using up all their energy worrying about how well they will do or by playing the game in their heads before it starts. Still others like assistance in boosting their confidence. They prefer to seek out a coach for some last minute counsel on strategy or for reassurance of their capability and readiness.

It is a coach's task to ascertain how each individual athlete should be treated while waiting to perform. It rarely works to unilaterally impose an identical pregame regimen for the entire team.

A good way to assess your athletes' beliefs and desires regarding optimal pregame routines is simply to ask them what they feel works best for them. You still may have to educate them, and otherwise help them sort out what really does aid performance from superstitions regarding what works; but with such questioning, at least you can find out what they want, and what they are likely to resist.

Routine Routines

Obviously, even if you manage to accurately assess each individual athlete's preference for a pregame routine, you will not want them all to follow through on their preferred approach. As already mentioned, some athletes will have acquired superstitious beliefs that routines which are truly deleterious work. You don't want them to continue to go through such pregame nonsense. (Though there are many superstitious routines that serve to help athletes relax and therefore truly are effective.) Nor can you allow them their preferred routines if such routines interfere with the team's performance. You must do what is best for the team.

For example, some athletes might find that they do better if they escape into their stereo headphones until their time to compete. If other members of the team are competing in turn, you might want to allow some exception for athletes prone to performance-debilitating anxiety, but wish the majority of the team to cheer and otherwise lend support to their teammates. They can't do that if they are lost in their music.

Some athletes tend to assuage their pre-competitive fears and doubts by verbalizing them. If it works for them, it's not too bad (though it is much better to directly confront and obliterate such negative thinking). But if such talk comes within earshot of teammates it can be contagious. It may evoke similar fears and doubts that do not get handled as effectively.

Some athletes try to raise their confidence levels by putting others down. That is by no means the confidence builder of choice. And you certainly don't want your athletes belittling their teammates or getting ready at each other's expense.

Pregame routines are important components of championship performances and should be explicitly discussed in a team meeting or classroom session. When you do, it is helpful to cite specific examples of what has been done on your team and what effects it seemed to have on that individual and the rest of the team. Then as a team, you can come up with pregame routines that will optimize *both* individual and team readiness.

THE MISSED CHAMPIONSHIP

Follow The Leader

Your athletes will make mistakes. The team will suffer setbacks in the pursuit of excellence. Opportunities and championships will be squandered and lost. When they are, how do you handle them?

Do you stay goal-oriented, realizing that what is done cannot be changed, and go about the business of getting back on course? Or do you kick yourself or chastise your athletes?

How do you want your athletes to handle the mistakes and the setbacks they encounter on the road to excellence? Are you modeling the manner in which you want them to respond to errors, setbacks and defeat? Or are you stuck in the fantasy world of "do what I say, not what I do?"

"It's Okay Coach, I Tried"

After a poor performance does an athlete need to show that he tried in order for it (or him) to be okay? Does he need to demonstrate that he cares that he lost? Should he be remorseful: "I'm sorry coach. I tried, but I just couldn't get him." Does he have to graphically demonstrate that he's exhausted, he gave all he could possibly give? Should he be sad, and perhaps cry (after all, immediately following a defeat is about the only moment a male athlete is permitted to cry)? Or, maybe he should be angry? He could cuss, throw equipment, kick the ground, slap the water or wrap his golf club around the nearest tree. How else is a coach to know that he really wanted to win?. . .Or, now that it is over and the results of the game must stand, does it really matter?

No Kid Gloves For Athletes' Tears

When athletes do poorly, many of them overreact and get down about their performance. It surely is disappointing for them to point toward the contest and then come up short of their goals. But it is not the end of the world, and they do not need to act as if it is. Nor do you or teammates need to support such overreaction.

Athletes do not need to be consoled or treated with kid gloves after a failure. Doing so only makes a bigger deal of the consequences stemming from the lost opportunity than truly exist.

Athletes do not need to feel badly after a disappointing performance. But if they do, you do not need to worry about it or deal with it. If they want to cry or mope, you don't have to rescue them. It's okay if they hurt a little. They are not going to die. They are not that fragile.

You might want to ask athletes, however, to take their gloom elsewhere. You don't want their dark clouds to shade the team climate, or adversely affect others' performance expectations. Tell them to get it out of their systems and come back ready to contribute to the team's mission.

Shouldering The Burden

It's tremendously frustrating to work so hard toward capturing the championship, then have so little control at the moment of truth. You guide the trip and, depending on the sport, may have the opportunity to make the decisions and call the plays, but the athletes play the game. No matter how much you'd like to be in there, you only get to watch.

So those times when the team fails to capture the championship, it can be mighty easy to point the finger of blame at those who were playing. Blame, however, won't give you the championship ring that has already been captured by the other team. In fact, blame won't help at all. Other opportunities, however, are best served by judiciously assigning responsibility to the person in charge. As Joe Paterno says, "If we lose,...that's my responsibility as a head coach....After all, I have more control of the game than the players. I have to prepare them....Sure, the players on the field do or don't make the big play but it's my job to give them the tools to win."[57]

THE CAPTURED
CHAMPIONSHIP

Shrugging The Spotlight

As mentioned earlier, coaching is a helping profession. In sports, help is conferred from the sidelines. Often it best remains there. You might come out to shield your athletes from criticism, but when it comes time for applause, stay in the shadows and push your team forward.

When offering his philosophy of coaching, the winningest football coach ever, Paul "Bear" Bryant, suggested that, "There's just three things I ever say. If anything goes bad, then I did it. If anything goes semi-good, then we did it. If anything goes real good, then you did it. That's all it takes to get people to win football games for you."[58]

The Never Ending Quest

When afforded too much emphasis, the captured championship can put a damper on athletic performance. Far too many athletes have arrived at the pinnacle of their sport, experienced the fleeting thrill of goal achievement, and then looked around only to find, as Gertrude Stein once said about Oakland, "When you get there, there isn't any there." Then, motivation can wane or, even worse, depression and attrition set in.

Meanwhile, the captured championship cannot be viewed as the end of the road. If an athlete has achieved the ultimate, what's left for which to strive? Nor should you allow your athletes ever to be satisfied. Excellence is nurtured by success without satisfaction.

Track coach John Anderson repeatedly talked to his charge David Moorcroft "about no performance being the end, but only a part of the pursuit of still better ones." Anderson suggests that, "The philosophy of never being satisfied and the *practice* of running fast combine to reject the logic of just running to win and get you on toward perfection."[59]

The Continuing Challenge

The captured championship can be the thrill of a lifetime for all involved. It can be, but hopefully it is not. It seems awfully sad for young athletes to have already had the highlights of their lives pass while most of their lives still lie before them.

The excitement generated by a captured championship need not be suppressed. Encourage your athletes to celebrate and enjoy their victory. But help them to recognize that at best the thrill of victory is fleeting. Instill in your athletes the value of the chase; for it is the process, not the product of the quest, that makes sport so meaningful and rewarding. That process can continue. The thrill inherent in the pursuit of excellence can go on and on.

CONCLUSION

The Pursuit Of Obsolescence

As a coach you are in many ways in the business of putting yourself out of business, or at least of striving to minimize the contribution you need to make to your athletes' performance. The better you do your job, the more completely your athletes learn their lessons. Ideally you teach them to prepare for and handle the pressures and demands of athletic competition on their own.

Shortly after runner David Moorcroft's 5,000 meter world record performance, his coach John Anderson supposed that Dave could "go on perfectly well without me." To instill that independence, Anderson observed, "That's the greatest coaching success of all."[60] ... And, that might very well be what coaching excellence is all about.

NOTES

1. Quoted in Kirkpatrick, Curry, "Wise in the ways of the wizard." Sports Illustrated, Nov. 30, 1981, Vol. 55, No. 23, p. 11.
2. Quoted in Callahan, Tom, "No. 1, and Still Counting." Time, Dec. 7, 1981, Vol. 118, No. 23, p. 68.
3. Quoted in Hyman, Mervin D. & White, Gordon S. Jr. Joe Paterno: "Football My Way." New York: Macmillan, 1971, p. 50.
4. Weaver, Earl, Winning. New York: Morrow, 1972, p. 185.
5. Quoted in Libby, Bill, The Coaches. Chicago: Henry Regner Company, 1972, p. 117.
6. Quoted in Moore, Kenny, "As We Join Our Show, Steve is, As Usual, Running." Sports Illustrated, June 22, 1981, Vol. 54, No. 26, p. 43.
7. Quoted in Phillips, B.J. "Football's supercoach." Time, Sept. 29, 1980, Vol. 116, No. 13, p. 71.
8. Quoted in Fimrite, Ron, "He's hired to be fired." Sports Illustrated, April 13, 1981, Vol. 54, No. 16, p. 55.
9. Libby, pp. 2-3.
10. Libby, p. 65.
11. Libby, p. 311.
12. Bell, Keith, Target On Gold. Austin, Tx: Keel Publications, 1983, p. 27.
13. Quoted in Deford, Frank, "The Rabbit Hunter." Sports Illustrated, Jan. 19, 1981, Vol. 54, No. 4, p. 68.
14. Deford, "Hunter." p. 68.
15. Libby, p. 127.
16. Halas, George, Halas by Halas. New York: McGraw Hill, 1979, p. 313.
17. Mitchell, Bobby, "'And You Dream About Tomorrow.'" Sports Illustrated, March 21, 1983, Vol. 58, No. 12, p. 83.
18. Hyman & White, p. 45.
19. Quoted in Moore, Kenny, "To Baffle and Amaze." Sports Illustrated, July 26, 1982, Vol. 57, No. 4, pp. 63-64.
20. Phillips, p. 73.
21. Hyman & White, p. 43.
22. Quoted in DeFord, Frank, "A man for all seasons." Sports Illustrated, Feb. 15, 1982, Vol. 56, No. 7, p. 61.
23. DeFord, "Seasons." p. 60
24. Quoted in Banks, Jimmy, The Darrell Royal Story. Austin, Tx.: Shoal Creek Publishers, 1973.
25. Rashad, Ahmad as told to Frank DeFord, Sports Illustrated, Oct. 18, 1982, Vol. 57, No. 17, p. 44.
26. Rashad, pp. 54-55.

27. Rashad, p. 52.
28. Hyman & White, p. 45.
29. Quoted in Swift, E.M. "This Coach Is First Class." Sports Illustrated, March 7, 1983, Vol. 58, No. 10, p. 61.
30. Swift, p. 64.
31. Quoted in Kirkpatrick, Curry, "Hallelujah, He's, Uh, Bum." Sports Illustrated, Oct. 27, 1980, Vol. 53, No. 18, p. 78.
32. Quoted in Lax, Eric, "Interview: Tom Lasorda." Sport, Oct. 1980, Vol. 71, No. 4, p. 22.
33. Quoted in Fimrite, Ron, "His Enthusiasm Is Catching." Sports Illustrated, April 4, 1983, Vol. 58, No. 14, p. 54.
34. Fimrite, "Enthusiasm." p. 54.
35. Quoted in Oates, Bob, The Winner's Edge, Fairfield, Iowa: Christopher, Maclay & Co. 1980, p. 187.
36. Hyman & White, p. 47.
37. Kirkpatrick, "Wise." p. 105.
38. Libby, p. 17.
39. Hyman & White, p. 29.
40. Moore, "Baffle." p. 72
41. Phillips, p. 72.
42. Hyman & White, p. 46.
43. Phillips, p. 73.
44. Fimrite, "Hired." p. 55.
45. Hyman & White, p. 45.
46. Hyman & White, p. 44.
47. Libby, p. 98.
48. Quoted in Brondfield, Jerry, Rockne. New York: Random House, 1976, p. 152.
49. Hyman & White, p. 50.
50. Phillips, p. 76.
51. Kirkpatrick, "Wise." p. 114.
52. Phillips, p. 77.
53. Bell, Keith, Winning Isn't Normal. Austin, Tx: Keel Publications, 1982, p. 8.
54. Hyman & White, p. 26.
55. Hyman & White, p. 25.
56. Libby, p. 141.
57. Hyman & White, p. 26.
58. Phillips, p. 74.
59. Quoted in More, Kenny, "'What Made Him Go So Wonderfully Mad?'" Sports Illustrated, Feb. 16, 1983, Vol. 58, No. 7, p. 83.
60. Moore, "Mad." p. 78.

ABOUT THE AUTHOR

DR. KEITH BELL is an internationally known sports psychologist, coach and athlete, He received his Ph.D. in 1974 from the University of Texas. Since then, he has helped thousands of coaches and athletes perform better and enjoy their sport more through his seminars, speaking engagements, consultations, and publications.

Dr. Bell has coached NCAA, club, and masters swimming teams, runners, and triathletes. In 1988 he was named U.S.M.S. Swimming Coach of the Year. An NCAA, masters, and long-distance swimmer, Dr. Bell has won numerous world and national swimming titles, He presently ranks among the fastest masters swimmers in the world.

──── ORDER FORM ────

KEEL PUBLICATIONS
P.O. Box 200575-CX
Austin, Texas 78720-0575

Send me the following books today!

_____copies of **CHAMPIONSHIP SPORTS PSYCHOLOGY**   @ $ 21.95

_____copies of The Nuts & Bolts of **PSYCHOLOGY FOR SWIMMERS**   @ $ 11.95

_____copies of **WINNING ISN'T NORMAL**   @ $ 10.95

_____copies of Target on Gold: **GOAL SETTING FOR SWIMMERS**
                              and Other Kinds of People   @ $ 8.95

_____copies of **SWIMMING PSYCHOLOGY**   @ $ 19.95

_____copies of **PSYCHOLOGY FOR SWIMMING COACHES**   @ $ 19.95

_____copies of **COACHING EXCELLENCE**   @ $ 19.95

NAME _____

ADDRESS _____

CITY_____ STATE_____ ZIP _____

Shipping: Add $1.75 for the first book and 75¢ for each additional book.

Texas residents please add 6% sales tax.

_____ I can't wait 3-4 weeks for Book Rate. Here is $3.50 per book for Air Mail.

Enclosed is my check for total of: $_____